D E A D
RECKONING

---◆---

C A L C U L A T I N G
WITHOUT INSTRUMENTS

D E A D
RECKONING
◆
C A L C U L A T I N G
WITHOUT INSTRUMENTS

RONALD W. DOERFLER

Gulf Publishing Company
Houston, London, Paris, Zurich, Tokyo

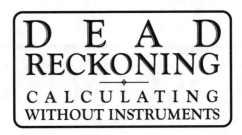

DEAD
RECKONING
◆
CALCULATING
WITHOUT INSTRUMENTS

ISBN 0-88415-087-9

Gulf Publishing Company
Book Division
P.O. Box 2608 ☐ Houston, Tx 77252-2608

10 9 8 7 6 5 4 3 2 1

Library of Congress Catalog Card Number

Doerfler, Ronald W.
    Dead reckoning : calculating without instruments / Ronald W. Doerfler.
        p. cm.
    Includes bibliographical references and index.
    ISBN 0-88415-087-9
    1. Ready-reckoners. I. Title.
QA11.D64   1993   93-12481
513'.9—dc20   CIP

For Eilish, Derek, and Matthew

Contents

Acknowledgment ix

1. A Time for Reckoning 1

2. Primitives 9
   Addition and Subtraction, 9
   Multiplication, 10
   Division, 19
   The Greatest Common Divisor, 35
   Error-Checking and Divisibility Tests, 39
   Factorization, 47
   A Factoring Game, 68

3. Roots.. 77
   Roots of Perfect Powers, 77
   Particular Square Root Methods, 79
   The Chebyshev Correction, 86
   A General Square Root Algorithm, 87
   The Reciprocal Square Root, 97
   Cube Roots, 99
   Higher-Order Roots, 105

4. Logarithms and Their Inverses 113

General Logarithmic Approximations, 116
Neighboring Value Relations, 121
Intermediate Value Relations, 123
An Iterative Relation, 130
Approximate Logarithmic Inverses, 133
An Example Problem, 142

5. Trigonometric Functions and Their Inverses 145

Sine and Cosine Functions, 146
The Tangent Function, 152
The Arcsine and Arccosine Functions, 156
The Arctangent Function, 161
Other Approximations, 165

6. Concluding Remarks 167

Appendix: Finding Rational Approximations to Precomputed Constants 171

Index 179

Acknowledgment

I would like to thank my family for their support throughout the years for pursuits such as this one. My parents, George and Barbara, are responsible for promoting the type of education that provides variety and interest to me, as well as the physical activities that provide equivalent satisfaction. My wife, Eilish, has always been interested in my often unusual undertakings, and I appreciate the many opportunities to share my ideas on them with her. Finally, I want to acknowledge the contributions of my two sons, Derek and Matthew; the image of them reading this book some years from now guided me in writing in the clearest, most honest manner that I can.

A Time for Reckoning

The human mind, when it sails by dead reckoning, without the possibility of a fresh observation, perhaps without the instruments necessary to take one, will sometimes bring up in very strange latitudes.

James Russell Lowell (1890), "Witchcraft" [1]

If the mind with its hundred billion neurons is the most intricate amalgam in the known universe, we should expect to do marvelous things with it. As we form electrical pathways among the hundred trillion synapses in the mind when performing a task, or even in anticipating a task, a library of pertinent mind maps and templates would be invaluable. This book investigates a portion of such a library, a shelf in the mathematics section, and browsing there can be an enjoyable and interesting experience for us.

This book describes techniques of computation and approximation that may be used to rapidly and mentally calculate mathematical quantities, including results of arithmetic operations and values of elementary functions. Some of these methods are very old, some are relatively recent, and some are new. Overall, the idea is to enjoy developing these capabilities. The concept of dead

1

reckoning is meant to convey the adventurous and challenging spirit that I perceive in this pursuit. At the very least, we will experience a portion of the panorama of elementary mathematics that mankind has had thousands of years to develop and that includes many calculational methods, of which we normally consider the ones we learned in school to be the only (or even best) ones. For mental calculations, they usually are not. An analogous situation occurred in the development of our present pen-and-paper methods of calculation that minimize erasures, supplanting the ancient sand reckoning methods in which digits were continuously and instantly erased and overwritten in the course of the calculations.

This does not pretend to be a book for teaching arithmetic. It is intended for those in high school, college, or professional occupations who are intrigued by mathematics, regardless of whether they are considered "good" at it or not. Unlike some books on calculational shortcuts, it is not a business math book— you won't find any dollar signs here. No exercises are included; the world is full of them. On the other hand, this book is replete with examples, which usually offer more personal insight than the often forbidding symbolic formulas.

For those who appreciate numbers and their interrelationships, the ability to perform mental calculations can provide a great deal of personal satisfaction and recreation. Speed is without a doubt a major objective of these techniques, but the sheer power of the mind to extract, say, square roots to sixteen or more digits offsets, I feel, the several minutes required for someone of my limited capabilities to do it. Therefore, speed is not the only concern and some methods are included that do take some time. Some of these algorithms are very interesting and can be thought-provoking in their own right.

Some may say that this book is a relic, given the calculating power available to anyone these days. I counter that the contents of this book are in fact both timeless and timely. Certainly the enjoyment of exploring mathematics and the challenge of stretching our personal capabilities will always exist for a cognitive people. On the other hand, I propose that this is a very appropriate time for presenting such calculational methods, for two curiously interrelated reasons. First, the proliferation of electronic calculators and computers throughout our lives and educational systems are eliminating calculational techniques from our memory and from our children's education, threatening to dim our already narrow view of this very rich field.

Ironically, the material in this book is also timely because a substantial amount of work on fast calculational algorithms was performed in the early days of mechanical and electronic computers. Limited in speed and memory and structured as sequential operations (sound familiar?), these early computers demanded simple, fast, and accurate approximations to mathematical functions. The work in this field, particularly that for decimal machines, is reflected in a variety of techniques gathered and presented in this book. Notably, more recent work in computer algorithms is much less significant; numeric coprocessors, extended-bit precision, parallel processing, and so forth have made the results much less applicable to humans. Newer algorithms, such as the Fast Fourier Transform (FFT) method of multiplication, often rely on internal architectures of microprocessors and their siblings, arrays of available memory locations, and/or inherent bit-shifting operations, none of which find analogy in our thought processes.

My own inability to readily approximate elementary functions was first brought home several years ago while I was working in an engineering laboratory. I required the value of sin 28° to quickly check a test result. Not having a calculator with me, I came to the shocking realization that, excluding the tedium of calculating terms by hand in the slowly converging Maclaurin power series (in radian units, no less), I was lost. Throughout my physics and mathematics education, trigonometric functions were always found from tables, slide rules, or calculators.

The next day, as it turned out, the need arose in a meeting to estimate the square root of 39. Again, a ready estimate to any significant accuracy at all was impossible. I was appalled.

I was determined to do something about this. As a graduate teaching assistant I had quietly enjoyed calculating results of arithmetic expressions before students could locate their calculators, and I felt I had a fair aptitude with numbers. I had recently read Steven B. Smith's excellent book, *The Great Mental Calculators* [2], and was somewhat relieved to recall that these were not feats that calculating prodigies were generally capable of doing either. Trigonometric functions were definitely not their province, and non-integer roots were seldom attempted.

Let us digress here for a moment to talk about such prodigies, as we will occasionally encounter them in the later chapters. At the outset, I would like to make it clear that I am not one of these lightning calculators, a very talented and practiced breed. However, it also seems appropriate in these days of high-speed pocket calculators to add that despite popular notions, these lightning calculators, which we can certainly strive to emulate, were and are by no means instantaneous in deriving their results. Due to the paucity of reliable measurements of response times, as well as the large deviations evident among specific types of presentations and calculators, I am extremely reluctant to elaborate on this and refer the interested reader to Smith's detailed exposition. I would like to caution that descriptions of performances by lightning calculators are poor yardsticks. They are generally written to flatter the calculator, they ignore such delay tactics as conversation and writing or repeating numbers, and they arbitrarily use phrases such as "in an instant," "in a flash," "momentarily," and so forth, which are not quantified.

With this established up front, and only to demonstrate the finite time required, I point out a test, better than most, reported in 1894 by Alfred Binet. In the test, the time required to multiply 6241 by 3635 ranged from 21 seconds (Jacques Inaudi) to 70.5 seconds (Ugo Zaneboni). Pericles Diamandi took 127 seconds to multiply 8637 by 4538. On the other hand, Johann Dase was credited by a knowledgeable observer in 1861 with mentally multiplying two eight-digit numbers (79532853 and 93758479) correctly in 54 seconds. It is also true that two-digit by two-digit multiplications are often immediately drawn, at least with very little adjustment, from memory.

Equally important is the realization that the results are not generated by a spontaneous process. From Hofstadter [3]:

From such people's introspection, as well as from extensive research by psychologists, it has been ascertained that nothing occult takes place during the performances of lightning calculators, but simply that their minds race through intermediate steps with the kind of self-confidence that a natural athlete has in executing a complicated motion quickly and gracefully. They do not reach their answers by some sort of instantaneous flash of enlightenment (though, subjectively, it may feel that way to some of them), but—like the rest of us— by sequential calculation . . .

Mental calculators have usually been extremely talented individuals who mastered their craft through sheer diligence from an early age. Efforts typically involved memorization of large tables, including two-digit endings for root extraction, logarithmic tables, factors of large numbers, and powers of two-digit numbers. Coupled with an innate number sense cultivated over years, the calculator historically provided astonishing feats of computation of limited types, often without an explicit algebraic understanding of the techniques. On the other hand, many noted theoreticians were considered lightning calculators, including Pascal, Gauss, Euler, Ampere, Wallis (who purposefully developed the ability in middle age), Aitken, Fermi, and Von Neumann.

Actually, the types of calculations performed by professional lightning calculators are often specialized to a degree that one would rarely encounter them even in technical work. These include extracting higher roots of exact powers, finding multiple squares whose sum is given (for example, every integer can be expressed as at least one sum of four squares), calculating compound interest, and performing day–date calendar functions.

I began, then, to survey the methods of lightning calculators as well as what I discovered to be a rather extensive field in numerical analysis, approximation of elementary functions. This was simply an interest of mine initially. After a couple of years, I decided to write an article for a mathematics journal. However, the article grew quite large and the scope eventually widened to culminate in this book instead. I am quite sure that you will not find another book like this one; I looked and ended up researching this one.

This book is aimed at those of us who, through our interest in mathematics, have acquired a general appreciation for numbers (i.e., a number sense), but have limited desire, time, or talent to develop the tools of lightning calculators. While the techniques and strategies presented are amenable to mental calculation, they are useful, of course, for quick pen-and-paper calculations as well.

Ideally, I think, algorithms designed to be performed mentally should have the following characteristics:

1. Multiplications that are limited to two-digit by three-digit at most
2. Divisions that are limited to two-digit divisors at most
3. A short-term memory requirement of no more than two numbers at any one time
4. A very minimum number of memorized table values
5. A relatively quick result, accurate to at least three digits, with the capability of extending this accuracy if so desired

This book, then, is not meant to provide a general collection of approximation techniques, but rather to merge selected tools of the mental calculator with relatively modern techniques of numerical analysis. To be precise, it is comprised of a set of useful methods and algorithms for rapidly and mentally finding products, quotients, roots of nonperfect powers, trigonometric values, and logarithmic and exponential values. Extremely detailed error analyses are omitted here to preserve the flavor of the discussion (and, to be honest, my taste for the subject). If you are interested in more detail, please consult the references cited; I have tried to be meticulous. Brief derivations of formulas, however, are generally given as they occur, although I trust the mathematicians among us will forgive my lack of rigor.

A notation mention is unavoidable here, because in this book certain operations involve working with groups of digits in a number. The notation $|\mathbf{n}$ represents a two-digit number string; if more digits exist in $\mathbf{n}$, they are "melded," or added, to the digits to the left of the "$|$" sign. For example, $3|129 = 4|29 = 429$. We simply want to work with hundreds groups in the number, and these can carry or borrow as needed from neighboring groups.

Don't be confused by the fact that there are three digits in the rightmost hundreds group of $3|129$. This can occur in an intermediate result of calculating with individual groups; the melding process returns each hundreds group to two digits. To illustrate, consider the numbers 184 and 245. To add these, we can split them up into two-digit groupings ($1|84$ and $2|45$) and add each piece separately ($1|84 + 2|45 = 3|129$). We then meld the result into the final answer:

$$\begin{array}{r} 3 \\ +\ 129 \\ \hline 429 \end{array}$$

where the 1 is a carry into the group on its left, as in addition. While this notation may seem unnecessary at this point, we will find that in multiplication, division, and square root extraction, we can work comfortably with separate two-digit groups within numbers and then meld the final answer back to a number with two-digit groupings, whence we drop the vertical bars.

It often turns out that when we work with individual groups in a calculation, one or more groups ends up as a negative number. In the same way that we "carried" a 1 in melding 3 | 129 into 4 | 29, we can borrow a 1 from a group to add 100 to the group to its right, as in subtraction. As an example, consider the calculation 54221 − 10536. We break the original numbers into two-digit groupings (5 | 42 | 21 and 1 | 05 | 36) and perform the subtraction on each piece separately, arriving at 4 | 37 | −15 = 4 | 36 | (100 − 15) = 4 | 36 | 85 = 43685.

We will occasionally encounter a situation where we want to work with three-digit, or thousands, groupings in a number. To distinguish three-digit groupings, we can employ the comma as the separator, since commas generally separate thousands groupings with numbers anyway. The final melding process reduces the number to positive three-digit groupings by carrying or borrowing as before from groups to the left. For example, 217,39,2820 = 217,039,2820 = 217,041,820 = 217041820. The group 39 was expanded to 039 to fill its grouping; remember, these are *separate* three-digit numbers until they are melded:

$$\begin{array}{r} 217 \\ 039 \\ 2820 \\ \hline 217041820 \end{array}$$

Rarely, we will need to indicate single-digit groupings. I have chosen a double vertical bar (| |) as the separator. To illustrate, we will show later that multiplying a two-digit number **ab** by 11 gives a result **a** | | **(a + b)** | | **b**, so

11 × 78 = 7 | | (7 + 8) | | 8 = 7 | | 15 | | 8 = 8 | | 5 | | 8 = 858

It quickly becomes very easy to meld groups into a final answer in a left-to-right manner as the answer is being read out. Do you see that 2 | 145 | –35 | 4 | –3 = 344650397?

The examples in this book have been chosen to provide realism to the presentation. Although it is impossible to select numbers that do not have some sort of special property in an application, I have endeavored to select values that are not particularly special (but, ironically, are then atypical). In a few cases I have deliberately chosen a value demonstrating the particular advantage of a certain technique. Where a special characteristic of a number does appear, as in that case, I have attempted to point it out. I have no interest in distorting the efficacy of the methods in this book. In practice we usually find that shortcuts abound.

It may appear in some instances that the results are taken to extreme accuracy. However, it is my experience that results to lesser accuracy become easy only when ones to higher accuracy are attempted. Too, a good deal of personal enjoyment can be had in pursuing a calculation to our best efforts. Finally, this enables us to judge the capabilities of various techniques.

A mathematics professor of mine once told me that he was surprised occasionally in calculus, rarely in trigonometry, and never in algebra. I wonder if he would be surprised by some of the arithmetic in this book.

Bibliography

1. James Russell Lowell, *Among My Books Vol. I*, Houghton, Mifflin and Co., Boston, 1904, p. 182.
2. Steven B. Smith, *The Great Mental Calculators*, Columbia University Press, New York, 1983.
3. Douglas R. Hofstadter, *Gödel, Escher, Bach: An Eternal Golden Braid*, Basic Books, New York, 1979, p. 567.

Primitives

The whole of Mathematics consists in the organization of a series of aids to the imagination in the process of reasoning.

Alfred North Whitehead (1898) [1]

"Primitive" methods are those strategies for performing arithmetic operations such as addition, subtraction, multiplication, and division, as well as the means of error checking the results. These have been culled from a number of sources, some of which provide them as particular "tricks" without an appreciation of the extensions necessary for developing general tools. My intention is to describe methods useful in a variety of calculations; excluded are tricks specific to certain numbers (except for divisibility tests) or uncommon digit distributions within numbers. The techniques in this chapter, aside from their intrinsic value, form helpful tools for mentally calculating the functions elsewhere in the book.

Addition and Subtraction

Addition and subtraction offer little, actually, in shortcuts. In general, it is a great help to mentally group digits into twos or threes for the same reason that it is easier to add 49.55 to 39.62 than 4,955 to 3,962. As mentioned in Chapter 1, the notation

9

a | b denotes the digits **a** followed by the digits **b**, where **b** is reduced to two digits by melding higher digits into **a**. In the above example,

$$4955 + 3962 = 49|55 + 39|62$$
$$= 88|117$$
$$= 89|17$$
$$= 8917$$

Also, $4955 - 3962 = 10|-7 = 9|93 = 993$. The usefulness of this notation will become apparent later.

It is often convenient to adjust the numbers for simplicity:

$$688 + 443 = 700 + 443 - 12$$

$$1514 - 688 = 1514 - 700 + 12$$

Some authors contend that one should never subtract per se, but rather think of adding a number to the subtrahend to get the minuend on a digit by digit, or in our case a group by group, basis.

$$
\begin{array}{r}
4\ 9\ 5\ 5 \\
-\ ^{13\,1}9\ 6\ 2 \\
\hline
9\ 9\ 3
\end{array}
\qquad
\begin{array}{l}
2 + 3 = 5 \\
6 + 9 = 15,\ \text{carry 1 to subtrahend} \\
9 + 1 + 9 = 19,\ \text{carry 1 to subtrahend} \\
3 + 1 + 0 = 4
\end{array}
$$

or,

$$39|62 + 10|-7 = 49|55$$

What is apparent here is that these methods all boil down to the same thing in slightly different ways. Believe me, though, it is the way we think about the numbers that can make them seem easy to calculate. This is particularly true in the multiplication routines.

Multiplication

Splitting numbers into groups, or using "group vision" as Menninger [2] calls it, is also useful in multiplications. For example, to multiply a number by 5 we halve ten times the number. This halving process is eased if we advantageously split up the number into groups of even numbers:

$$5629432 \times 5 = 56 \ 2 \ 94 \ 32 \ 0 \div 2$$

$$= 28147160$$

Mental calculators often performed multiplication as a series of additions according to the Distributive Law of Algebra:

$$386 \times 471 = 300 \bullet 400 + 300 \bullet 70 + 300 \bullet 1$$

$$+ \ 80 \bullet 400 + 80 \bullet 70 + 80 \bullet 1$$

$$+ \ 6 \bullet 400 + 6 \bullet 70 + 6 \bullet 1$$

with appropriate shortcuts thrown in (e.g., any calculator would complete two-digit multiplications almost instantly, shortening the steps). A digit by digit solution is possible by performing the classical multiplication routine vertically instead of horizontally, called cross multiplication [2]. To find 386×471:

$6 \bullet 1 = 6$

$6 \bullet 7 + 8 \bullet 1 = 0$, carry 5

$6 \bullet 4 + 8 \bullet 7 + 3 \bullet 1 + 5 = 8$, carry 8

$8 \bullet 4 + 3 \bullet 7 + 8 = 1$, carry 6

$3 \bullet 4 + 6 = 18$

Answer: 181806

While this eliminates the need to remember the intermediate values in the classical algorithm, the left-to-right nature of the first technique is better suited to writing the answer while it is being obtained. At least one contemporary lightning calculator uses two-digit by two-digit multiplications in cross multiplication [3].

For those of us without the practiced rhythm necessary for quickly doing these steps, there are several ways of simplifying the calculation by manipulating the numbers into simpler ones. In fact, this is where the fun lies in all of this.

One way of simplifying a multiplication is to make use of the identity

$$(a + b) \bullet (a + c) = a(a + b + c) + bc \tag{1}$$

Therefore,

$$105 \times 117 = 122 \bullet 100 + 5 \bullet 17$$

$$98 \times 89 = 87 \bullet 100 + 2 \bullet 11$$

$$85 \times 117 = 102 \bullet 100 - 15 \bullet 17$$

$$= 10200 - (22 \bullet 10 + 5 \bullet 7)$$

or

$$= 10200 - (12 \bullet 20 + 3 \bullet 5)$$

It is impossible to adequately convey the usefulness and pervasiveness of this technique in practice; if you don't use it, do. Interestingly enough, this method was once taught to schoolchildren in lieu of teaching the multiplication tables above 5×5 [4]. To illustrate, the product 8×7 was found by forming this diagram:

$$\begin{array}{cc} 8 & 7 \\ \seardown & \swarrow \\ \swarrow & \searrow \\ 3 & 2 \quad 6 \\ \hline & 5 \end{array}$$

where the 2 and 3 are differences from 10 of 8 and 7, 5 is $7 - 2$ or $8 - 3$, and 6 is 3×2, giving 56 as the answer.

Why not? Perhaps a second-grader today should learn this technique instead of learning multiples of 12.

There is an analogous method in finger-counting that utilizes this relation as well. Again, to find the product 8×7, we begin with two closed fists. We then raise fingers on one hand to count from the first number 8 to 10, and we repeat this for the number 7 on the other hand. Then the sum of the closed fingers is the tens digit and the product of the raised fingers is the units digit.

We can also extend Equation 1 to cases where both numbers are near numbers of which one is a multiple **n** of the other. A straightforward approach would be to multiply the smaller number by **n**, use Equation 1, and then divide the result by **n**. An easier way makes use of the identity

$$(a + b) \bullet (na + c) = a[(na + c) + nb] + bc$$

$$36 \times 157 = 40(157 - 4 \bullet 4) + 4 \bullet 3$$

$$= 40 \bullet 141 + 12$$

$$= 5652$$

Again, **b** and **c** are signed quantities.

The last example also demonstrates a convenient tool, useful when a multiplier is divisible by 9:

$$36 \times 157 = (40 - 40/10) \bullet 157$$

$$= (1 - 1/10) \bullet 40 \bullet 157$$

$$= 62|80 - 6|28$$

$$= 5652$$

Of course, this is a special case of the common practice of multiplying by a nearby round number and correcting the result:

$$26 \times 87 = 26 \bullet 90 - 3 \bullet 26 = 23|40 - 78 = 2262$$

When multiplying two numbers **a5** and **b5** that end in 5, we might remember the relation,

$$(a5) \bullet (b5) = \left(ab + \frac{a + b}{2}\right)|25$$

$$35 \times 75 = (21 + 5)|25$$

$$= 2625$$

If $(a + b)$ is odd, the .5 emerging from the average is assumed to merge into the $|25$, producing $|75$.

$$65 \times 235 = (138 + 14)|75$$

$$= 15275$$

A final instance of algebraic manipulation to ease multiplications is given by D. E. Smith [5]:

$$(10a + a) \bullet (10b + b) = [(10a + a)b + ab] \bullet 10 + ab$$

$$22 \times 44 = (22 \bullet 4 + 2 \bullet 4) \bullet 10 + 2 \bullet 4$$

$$= 960 + 8 = 968$$

Other points to be aware of include

$$25 \times n = n|00 \div 4$$

$$75 \times n = 3n|00 \div 4$$

$$125 \times n = 8n,000 \div 8$$

$$15 \times n = (n + n/2) \bullet 10, \text{ or } (n/2) \bullet 3 \bullet 10$$

$$11 \times a||b = a||(a + b)||b$$

Here **b** is the units digit of a number, and **a** can contain one or more digits. Considering the last relation above, if we multiply $a||b$ by a multiple of 11, we can multiply $a||b$ by the multiple and continue as if multiplying by 11. I reluctantly include this rule, as $11n = 10n + 1$ anyway, but it may be useful yet. To repeat our earlier example,

$$22 \times 44 \rightarrow 11 \times 88 = 8||16||8 = 968$$

Notice that the middle digit is melded to become a single digit, as indicated by the double bar notation. For larger numbers,

$$44 \times 643 \rightarrow 11 \times 25 | 72$$

$$= 2 | 17 | 15$$

$$\begin{array}{r} + \quad 7 | 19 | 12 \\ \hline 2 \quad 8 \quad 2 \quad 9 \quad 2 \end{array}$$

This may be extended to include multiplication by, say, 111:

$$111 \times a | | b = a | [(a + b) \bullet 11] | | b$$

where the middle section is now melded to two digits.

Note that often we can factor a number into one or more of these convenient numbers. Conversely, for example, the number 37 can be represented as 111/4.

Squaring is an extremely important operation to perform mentally, mainly because ordinary multiplications can usually be simplified into a square and a much simpler multiplication. Fortunately, squares offer advantages to us.

Squares can be obtained by using Equation 1 to reduce the number of significant digits:

$$(32)^2 = 30 \bullet 34 + (2)^2$$

$$(185)^2 = 200 \bullet 170 + (15)^2 = 34000 + 225$$

$$= 34225$$

Numbers ending in 5 can be squared by a trivial result of Equation 1, often presented as a number trick:

$$(35)^2 = [3(3 + 1)] | 25$$

$$= 1225$$

Conversely, general multiplication can make use of squares as follows (called the rule of quarter squares and of very ancient origins) [5]:

$$38 \times 32 = (35)^2 - (3)^2$$

$$62 \times 74 = (68)^2 - (6)^2 = 70 \bullet 66 + 4 - 36$$

It's useful to me in getting the signs right to remember that the average number squared is larger than the individual numbers multiplied.

Another convenient tool is to use the relation

$$(a + b)^2 = a^2 + b[a + (a + b)]$$

$$(31)^2 = (30)^2 + (30 + 31)$$

$$(58)^2 = (60)^2 - 2(60 + 58)$$

The square of a multiple of 3 can be found by extracting $(3)^2 = 9$ out of the quantity squared and letting this equal $(10 - 1)$ [5]:

$$(3a)^2 = 10a^2 - a^2$$

$$(132)^2 = 10(44)^2 - (44)^2$$

$$= 1 | 93 | 60 - 19 | 36$$

$$= 17424$$

One of the few explicit "tricks" I find worth remembering is extremely useful for squaring numbers from about 30 to 70. The result is obtained by adding the difference **b** from 50 to 25 and appending $\mathbf{b}^2$, melded to two digits [2].

$$(58)^2 = (8 + 25) | 64 = 3264$$

$$(37)^2 = 12 | 169 = 1369$$

For squaring a number between about 400 and 600, add the difference from 500 to 250 and append the square of the last two digits melded to three digits:

$(531)^2 = 281,961$

$(564)^2 = 314,39 | 196$

$= 318,096$

Also, it is sometimes convenient to recall that when squaring a two-digit number ending in 1,

$(a | | 1)^2 = a^2 | | 2a | | 1$

where the 2a term is melded to a single digit. This follows from the expansion of $(10a + 1)^2$. In addition, when squaring a number ending in 25, as in $a | 25$ [2],

$(a | 25)^2 = 10(a^2 + a/2), 625$

$(725)^2 = 525,625$

This follows from the identity

$(100a + 25)^2 = 1000(10a^2 + 5a) + 625$

By this point we should be adept at mentally multiplying two-digit by two-digit numbers. As you may have guessed, the later discussions in this book assume this ability. I recommend in spare moments sequencing through the two-digit numbers and squaring each one. This actually takes little time. The purpose is not to memorize the results but rather to formulate general strategies for arriving at them quickly. Remember here that "particular" techniques are really more general than they appear, because operations on numbers near convenient ones can use the latter and be adjusted at the end for the difference. I think you will discover that there are many ways to skin these cats.

To cube a number, it is generally easier not to square and multiply, but rather to use the expansion

$(a + b)^3 = a^3 + b^3 + 3ab(a + b)$

For example,

$$(23)^3 = 8027 + 180 \bullet 23$$

$$= 8027 + 10(21 \bullet 20 - 2 \bullet 3)$$

$$= 8027 + 4140$$

$$= 12167$$

Failing outright simplification of a large multiplication, we can make use of the following identity, apparently first introduced in a more complicated binary format in 1962 [6,7]:

$$a \,|\, b \times c \,|\, d = ac \bullet 10^4 + [ac + bd - (a - b) \bullet (c - d)] \bullet 10^2$$

$$+ \, bd$$

$$6823 \times 4519 = 68 \bullet 45 \times 10^4 + (68 \bullet 45 + 23 \bullet 19$$

$$- \, 45 \bullet 26) \times 10^2 + 23 \bullet 19$$

$$
\begin{array}{rl}
= & 3060\,|\,00\,|\,00 \\
+ & 23\ \ 27\,|\,00 \\
+ & 4\,|\,37 \\
\hline
& 3083\,|\,31\,|\,37 = 30833137
\end{array}
$$

thereby getting an eight-digit result by evaluating the products of only three two-digit by two-digit numbers. The usual expansion requires four such products:

$$a \,|\, b \times c \,|\, d = ac \bullet 10^4 + (ad + bc) \bullet 10^2 + bd$$

Both equations become identical when squaring numbers.

Knuth [6] comments that this method, while apparently never used by lightning calculators, should make eight-digit by eight-digit mental calculations "reasonable" by nesting the procedure. Although it reduces the number of two-digit multiplications from 16 to 9, it does require temporary storage of a few numbers simultaneously, a trivial task for a machine but a difficulty for mortals.

Division

Division reveals difficulties in simplification, serving to deepen my suspicion that addition, subtraction, and multiplication are artifacts of God, while division is a construct of man. Nonetheless, some things can be done. Following an overview of the useful properties of repeating decimals, we will delve into strategies for reciprocals of one-digit and two-digit numbers and divisors near a multiple of 10 before tackling large divisors.

To begin, we discuss certain properties of repeating (sometimes called recurring) decimals, that is, those numbers with digits (usually lying to the right of the decimal point) that recur in repeated groups [8–10]. For example, $1/7 = 0.14285714285714\ldots$, demonstrating this property. It happens that for a fraction s/t, a repeating decimal group will occur if t has one or more prime factors other than 2 or 5. Otherwise, since 2 and 5 are prime factors of 10, an exact decimal value will result (e.g., $13/16 = 0.8125$). A prime number is a positive integer other than 1 that is divisible only by itself and 1, such as 2, 3, 5, 7, 11, 13, etc. When repeating groups do occur, they may follow initial non-repeating digits. However, awareness of the existence of these groups can save a good deal of effort.

A pertinent question at this point is how we determine the number of decimal places we need to either terminate the number completely or complete the first repeating group and, in the latter case, the number of digits in the repeating group. For a denominator t with prime factors of 2 and 5 only, the number of decimal places will equal the highest power of 2 or 5 contained in t. In our example above, $16 = 2^4 \cdot 5^0$, so the ratio $13/16$ terminates after the fourth decimal place. Some would say that a terminating decimal is actually a repeating one, spewing out zeros or nines to infinity. We will not label these as such, if only to simplify our terminology.

Unfortunately, there is no general rule for determining the recurring period of repeating decimals, although there are some useful properties of some cases. First, we can see that a group will begin repeating when, in long division, we arrive at a remainder that is the same as earlier in the division, whence the whole process starts repeating. Since there are only $(t - 1)$ different remainders possible for a divisor t, the repeating group cannot have a period greater than $(t - 1)$. Our first example of $t = 7$ illustrates a repeating group of length $(t - 1)$, as do such numbers as 17, 19, 23, 29, 47, 59, 61, and 97. The reciprocal of 97 is occasionally asked of lightning calculators [11].

It turns out that for reciprocals $1/t$ with t prime, the period of the repeating group, if not equal to $(t - 1)$, must be exactly divisible into $(t - 1)$. For example, for the fraction 1/43, the group period must equal 42, 21, 14, 7, 6, 3, or 2. For a prime t between 3 and 487, the period of $1/(t^n)$ equals t^{n-1} times that for $1/t$. Therefore, the repeating group of 1/49 contains $7 \cdot 6$ or 42 digits. The period of a fraction $s/(3^n)$ equals (3^{n-2}) digits.

For a reciprocal $1/t$ with t composite (nonprime, or factorable), we can sometimes break t into prime factors $2^a \cdot 5^b \cdot t_1 \cdot t_2 \cdot t_3 \cdot \ldots$, where t_1, t_2, t_3, $\ldots$ are all different and are greater than 5. Then the period of the repeating group will equal the lowest common multiple of the periods of the repeating groups for $1/t_1$, $1/t_2$, $1/t_3$, etc. Yielding to a heightened sense of apprehension, I offer the example of 1/73920. Here we may find by factorization methods discussed later that $t = 2^6 \cdot 5 \cdot 3 \cdot 7 \cdot 11$. The recurring periods of the last three factors are 1, 6, and 2, whose lowest common multiple 6 is the recurring period of $1/73920 = 0.000013528138528138528\ldots$, where we notice that the recurring group appears after six nonrepeating digits, 000013.

In addition, the recurring period for numbers which are factors of 9, 99, 999, etc. will equal the number of nines in the lowest such multiple. For example, $999,999 = 3 \cdot 3 \cdot 3 \cdot 7 \cdot 11 \cdot 13 \cdot 37$ yields 63 combinations as factors. Except for the six that are factors of 9, 99 or 999 (3, 11, 33, 37, 111, and 333), all have a recurring period of six digits, including the factors 7, 13, 21, 39, 63, 77, 91, and so on. Since 3 is a factor of 9, its reciprocal has a recurring period of one digit. The numbers 11 and 33 produce two-digit periods, and 37, 111, and 333 yield three-digit periods.

In another special case of a reciprocal $1/t$ where $t = 2^a \cdot 5^b \cdot t_1^n$ and t_1 is any prime between 5 and 487, the period of the repeating group equals that of $1/t_1$ multiplied by t_1^{n-1}. For 1/968, we have $t = 2^3 \cdot 11^2$ with a recurring period of $2 \cdot 11 = 22$ digits.

Now, for irreducible fractions s/t yielding groups of even periods and with t prime, corresponding digits of the first and second halves of the period add up to 9. Therefore, if we know that 1/7 yielded an even period (as it does since it is one of the ones noted for periods of length $(t - 1)$ earlier), we need only find the first three digits .142 to know the last three of the group as 857. Again, $3/7 = .428571 \ldots$ Of course, this halves the effort required to find or memorize the reciprocal of, say, 97 as well. Other fractions with even periods but with t nonprime often exhibit this phenomenon, but not always. They always will if no factor of t divides $(10^n - 1)$, for n a positive integer. If t is not divisible by 2, 3, or 5 and $1/t$ has a period of $(t - 1)$ digits, this situation will occur as well. Finally, for $t = a^p \bullet b^q \bullet \ldots$, where each multiplier is a distinct prime other than 2 or 5, halves will be complementary if and only if the periods for $1/a$, $1/b$, etc. contain the same power of 2.

Also, for any reciprocal $1/t$, the last digit of the repeating group will be 1 or 9 if the units digit of t is 9 or 1, respectively. If t is prime and the units digit is not 1 or 9, the last digit of the repeating group will be the same as the units digit of t. Therefore, the repeating group for $1/7$ must end in 7, so if we take the fraction to two digits, or .14, we immediately know that $1/7 = .142857 \ldots$

We turn now to the task of finding the decimal expansion of a reciprocal $1/t$. The process of long division, which we can end when a remainder is repeated in the course of the calculation, is the obvious approach. There is another method which is frequently more convenient, particularly if the period of the recurring group is large. We divide by long division until some digits are determined and a low remainder is found. Then we can multiply the entire quotient (including the fraction remainder/t) by the remainder, converting the fractional part to proper form. Any digits to the left of the decimal point are discarded. This process of multiplication can be repeated until the recurring group is found, with checks provided by our earlier observations. For example, let us consider the reciprocal of 43:

$$1/43 = .023 \tfrac{11}{43}$$

$$11/43 = 11(.023 \tfrac{11}{43}) = .253 \ 121/43 = .255 \ 35/43$$

$$11^2/43 = 11(.255 \tfrac{35}{43}) = 2.805 \ 385/43 = 2.813 \ 41/43$$

etc.

Then 1/43 = 0.023255813 . . . .
We haven't reached the end of a recurring group yet, and of course it may take 42 digits. We could have continued our initial long division further and found 1/43 = 0.0232558 6/43. On the other hand, we can continue to 1/43 = 0.023255813 41/43, either by long division or even better as the intermediate result from multiplying by elevens in the calculation given above. Here we can take our remainder as –2 (I find that authors of arithmetic methods often don't take arithmetic literally enough). Then

$$1/43 = .023255814 \; -2/43$$

$$-2/43 = -2(.023255814 \; -2/43) = -.046511628 \; +4/43$$

$$-2^2/43 = -2(.046511628 \tfrac{4}{43}) = +.093023256 \; -8/43$$

See the recurrence beginning in the last result, realizing that $6 - \tfrac{8}{43} = 5 \; \tfrac{35}{43}$? We find then that

$$1/43 = .\overline{023255813953488372093}$$

where the raised line indicates the recurring group.
If we don't care to work with the fractional parts at all, we can ignore them if we keep the digits to the left of the decimal point in each step [9]. These extra digits are then melded into the digits previously found. Again, 1/43 = 0.023 with a remainder of 11, which multiplies the numbers in each line:

```
.023
   253
     2805
.023255805 . . .
```

Here, however, we would not discover the more convenient remainder of –2 which, as we have seen, would greatly simplify finding the rest of the repeating group. For reciprocals of numbers such as 37, 27, 7, 11, or 13, for example, that have multiples one less or more than a power of 10, the remainder after division to this number of places will obviously be 1 or –1, respectively. Then since 37 • 27 = 999 and 7 • 11 • 13 = 1001, we know that

$1/37 = .\overline{027}$

$1/27 = .\overline{037}$

and since 11 • 13 = 143, 7 • 13 = 91, and 7 • 11 = 77, we find

$$
\begin{array}{c}
.143 \\
-\quad 143 \\
+\qquad 143 \\
\hline
\qquad\quad \text{etc.}
\end{array}
$$

$1/7 = .\overline{142857}$

$$
\begin{array}{c}
.091 \\
-\quad 091 \\
+\qquad 091 \\
\hline
\qquad\quad \text{etc.}
\end{array}
$$

$1/11 = .\overline{09}$

$$
\begin{array}{c}
.077 \\
-\quad 077 \\
+\qquad 077 \\
\hline
\qquad\quad \text{etc.}
\end{array}
$$

$1/13 = .\overline{076913}$

Now 43 is prime and we have found above that the period of the recurring group is 21, a factor of $(43 - 1)$. For **t**'s containing more digits, we can, with some luck in remainders, save a great deal of time with these methods.

For numbers whose reciprocals yield recurring groups of length $(t - 1)$, values of **s/t** with **s** > 1 contain the same recurring group with its digits cycled to perhaps a different starting position. This happens to be true for $1/(7)^2$ as well.

For example, we recall that 1/17 has a recurrent period of $(t - 1)$ and we can find its value through the previous techniques. We need only find the first eight digits, as the last eight are complementary.

$1/17 = .0588 \ 4/17$

$4/17 = 4(.0588\tfrac{4}{17}) = .2352 \ 16/17$

Then

$1/17 = \overline{0.0588235294117647}$

Here we also see that since **t** is prime with a units digit of 7, the last digit of the recurring group is also 7. Realizing this, we actually only needed to ascertain the first seven digits of the reciprocal.

Now, say we're interested in the value of 13/17. We found the decimal expansion of 1/17 fairly easily, so let's divide 13 by 17 to a couple of digits or multiply the first few digits of 1/17 (which we round off) by 13, giving 13 • 059 = 767. This implies that the recurring group begins with the digits 764 in 1/17, and we assert that

$$13/17 = .\overline{7647058823529411}$$

which is indeed true. Lightning calculators of the showmanship variety occasionally use a trick involving a reciprocal such as 1/7 to perform seemingly unbelievable multiplications. Through a confederate in the audience or some other contrived means, the first number is produced, in this case, 142857. Now, we know that $1/7 = .\overline{142857}$, so $142857 = 10^6(1/7) - 1/7 = (10^6 - 1)/7$. Therefore, any other number easily multiplies this artifical one. For example, a legitimate audience member volunteers the number 6297 as the multiplier. Then,

$$6297 \times 142857 = \frac{6297000000 - 6297}{7}$$

$$= \frac{6296993703}{7}$$

and the short division is also done mentally to arrive at the correct answer of 899570529. Beware.

Returning to our discussion, let us consider the general case of finding the decimal expansion of **s/t**, where **s** is not necessarily 1. First, we can round off the divisor in many instances by adjusting the remainder or dividend in each step of the usual division process. For evaluating 1241/78 = 15.910 . . . , for example, we can replace the divisor by 80 and correct each remainder by the errant amount:

124/80 = 1   remainder = 44 + 1 • 2 = 46

461/80 = 5   remainder = 61 + 5 • 2 = 71

710/80 = 9   remainder = –10 + 9 • 2 = 8

80/80 = 1   remainder = 0 + 1 • 2 = 2

etc.

Notice that in the third step we had to back up and increase the previous quotient digit 8 to 9 because the adjusted remainder ended up greater than the divisor 80. The frequency of this situation increases as the original and rounded numbers are more distant. For an original number ending in 9, this situation never occurs during the string of zeros following the significant digits in the dividend. Digits in the quotient are simply inserted (added to zero) into the dividend a number of places to the right given by the power of 10. In this case, it is convenient to divide both the divisor ending in **n** nines (adjusted to a number ending in **n** zeros) and the dividend by 10n. Then as the division progresses, each digit of the quotient is added to the dividend **n** places later. For example, in the reciprocal 1/29, we round 29 to 30 and divide this and the dividend by 10:

.03448275 . . .
_____
3).103448275 . . .

where we add each digit of the quotient, as it's obtained, to the dividend one place later.

Now in the situation where a fraction s/t has a denominator t of the form (10m – 1) for **m** an integer, that is, it ends in a 9, we can mechanize the previous method of division to speed the process [9]. We can think in terms of the following relations:

a_0 = s (not necessarily 1)
b_n = integer part of a_n/m
c_n = remainder of above
a_{n+1} = $10c_n + b_n$

Now b_n will consist of the digits of the quotient. The term c_n, the remainder when a_n is divided by m, may be written as $a_n \bmod m$, where c_n is said to be congruent to a_n with respect to the modulus m. Let us consider the fraction 1/29 again. Then $m = 3$ and we have the following sequence of steps:

a	b	c
1	0	1
10	3	1
13	4	1
14	4	2
24	8	0
8	2	2
22	7	1
17	5	2
etc.		

giving us as we ripple mentally through the rhythmic process:

1/29 = .03448275 . . .

For the fraction 19/29 we have

a	b	c
19	6	1
16	5	1
15	5	0
5	1	2
21	7	0

etc.

correctly giving 19/29 = 0.65517 . . . .

Any divisor ending in 3 will transform into one ending in 9 through multiplication of the numerator and denominator by 3.

For t of the form $(10m + 1)$ or in other words ending in 1, and for s not necessarily unity, we set $a_{n+1} = 10c_n - b_n$. However, since we can end up with negative values of b_n (which may be melded to obtain a correct result), we can ensure positive values by setting b_n to one less than a_n/m if m divides a_n without remainder. For 1/21 we have

a	b	c
1	0	1
10	4	2
16	7	2
13	6	1
4	1	2
19	9	1
1	0	1

and here we have the initial line repeated, revealing that

$$1/21 = .\overline{047619}$$

Notice that divisors ending in 7 can be converted to ones ending in 1 by multiplying the numerator and denominator by 3.

If we don't mind obtaining the digits in a right-to-left manner, we can use another method, given by Taylor [9]. For a denominator of the form $(10m - 1)$, we can add shifted terms multiplied by **m**, beginning with the numerator itself. Taylor gives the examples of

$$1/39 = \quad .\overline{025641} \qquad \text{and} \qquad 1/13 = 3/39 = \quad .\overline{076923}$$

$$
\begin{array}{r}
1 \\
4 \\
16 \\
64 \\
256 \\
1024 \\
+\ 4096 \\
\hline
..025641
\end{array}
\qquad\qquad
\begin{array}{r}
3 \\
12 \\
48 \\
192 \\
768 \\
+\ 3042 \\
\hline
...076923
\end{array}
$$

Taylor gives other methods suitable for very particular divisors (such as squares) that we will not consider here.

For divisors generally lying near a power of 10, the remainder can be also be adjusted while the entire dividend is divided by the power of 10 [2]. For example, for 129641/97 we can perform the division by 100 first:

129641/100 = **1296**   remainder = 41
new remainder = 3 • 1296 + 41 = 3929
      3929/100 = **39**   remainder = 29
new remainder = 3 • 39 + 29 = 146
      146/100 = **1**   remainder = 46
new remainder = 3 • 1 + 46 = 49

Therefore, 129641/97 = (1296 + 39 + 1) = 1336 with a remainder of 49. Of course the division process can be carried further into the region to the right of the decimal point.

For divisors that have a multiple that lies near a power of 10, the remainder can also be adjusted as in the previous method. The difference consists of multiplying the quotient in each step by the value of the multiple factor. To illustrate this, we can find the value of 4330463/332, where 1000 = 3 • 332 + 4.

      4330463/1000 = 4330   remainder = 463
new quotient = 3 • 4330 = **12990**
new remainder = 4 • 4330 + 463 = 17783
      17783/1000 = 17   remainder = 783
new quotient = 3 • 17 = **51**
new remainder = 4 • 17 + 783 = 851
      851/332 = 2   remainder = 187

Therefore, 4330463/332 = (12990 + 51 + 2) = 13043 with a remainder of 187.

Now let us consider a method of cross division, or Fourier Division, as proposed by Joseph Fourier (1768–1830), useful for calculations involving multidigit divisors [12-14]. If we are dividing C by A to get B, then $AB = C$ and

$$
\begin{array}{l}
A = \quad a_1 \mid a_2 \mid a_3 \mid a_4 \ldots \\
\times\, B = \quad \underline{b_1 \mid b_2 \mid b_3 \mid b_4 \ldots} \\
\qquad p_1 \mid q_1 \\
\qquad\quad p_2 \mid q_2 \\
\qquad\qquad p_3 \mid q_3 \\
\qquad\qquad\quad p_4 \mid q_4 \\
\qquad\qquad\qquad \cdots \\
C = \overline{c_1 \mid c_2 \mid c_3 \mid c_4 \ldots}
\end{array}
$$

where the partial products $p_n \mid q_n$ are formed by multiplications of **a** and **b** terms. In particular,

$$p_1 \mid q_1 = a_1 b_1$$

$$p_2 \mid q_2 = a_1 b_2 + a_2 b_1$$

$$p_3 \mid q_3 = a_1 b_3 + a_2 b_2 + a_3 b_1$$

or,

$$p_n \mid q_n = \sum_{k=1}^{n} a_k b_{n+1-k} \qquad n = 1, 2, 3, \ldots$$

where the Greek letter Σ (sigma) indicates the sum of the terms for **k** from 1 to **n** here. Also,

$$\mid c_n = \mid p_n + \mid q_{n-1} \text{ with } q_0 = 0$$

We are interested in solving for $\mathbf{B} = b_1 \mid b_2 \mid b_3 \ldots$ given $\mathbf{A}$ and $\mathbf{C}$:

$$b_1 = \frac{p_1 \mid q_1}{a_1} = \frac{c_1 \mid (c_2 - p_2)}{a_1}$$

$$= \frac{c_1 \mid c_2}{a_1} \text{ with a remainder } R_1 = \mid p_2$$

$$b_2 = \frac{p_2 \mid q_2 - a_2 b_1}{a_1} = \frac{R_1 \mid (c_3 - p_3) - a_2 b_1}{a_1}$$

$$= \frac{R_1 \mid c_3 - a_2 b_1}{a_1} ; R_2 = \mid p_3$$

$$b_3 = \frac{p_3 \mid q_3 - a_2 b_2 - a_3 b_1}{a_1}$$

$$= \frac{R_2 \mid (c_4 - p_4) - a_2 b_2 - a_3 b_1}{a_1}$$

$$= \frac{R_2 \mid c_4 - a_2 b_2 - a_3 b_1}{a_1} \; ; \; R_3 = \; \mid p_4$$

In general,

$$b_n = \frac{p_n \mid q_n - \displaystyle\sum_{k=2}^{n} a_n b_{n+1-k}}{a_1}$$

$$= \frac{p_n \mid (c_{n+1} - p_{n+1}) - \displaystyle\sum_{k=2}^{n} a_n b_{n+1-k}}{a_1}$$

$$= \frac{p_n \mid (c_{n+1}) - \displaystyle\sum_{k=2}^{n} a_n b_{n+1-k}}{a_1} - \frac{\mid p_{n+1}}{a_1}$$

and, defining the remainder R_n as $\mid p_{n+1}$,

$$b_n = \frac{R_{n-1} \mid c_{n+1} - \displaystyle\sum_{k=2}^{n} a_n b_{n+1-k}}{a_1} \; ; \; R_n = \; \mid p_{n+1}$$

As an example, consider the division of C = 42472482 by A = 874921. We consider two-digit operations here, although single-digit operations are possible after, say, a two-digit a_1 is split off as the divisor. Notice that for accuracy the remainders R_n are adjusted to give numerators which are less than $a_1/2$, occasionally resulting in negative values of **b**.

$$\frac{C}{A} = \frac{42\,|\,47\,|\,24\,|\,82}{87\,|\,49\,|\,21}$$

$$b_1 = \frac{42\,|\,47}{87} = 49; \ R_1 = -16$$

quotient thus far: 49

$$b_2 = \frac{-16\,|\,24 - 49 \bullet 49}{87} = \frac{-1576 - 49 \bullet 49}{87}$$

$$= - (46, R\ -25) = - 46 \ ; \ R_2 = 25$$

49 | –46

$$b_3 = \frac{25\,|\,82 - (-46) \bullet 49 - 49 \bullet 21}{87} = 44 \ ; \ R_3 = -21$$

49 | –46 | 44

$$b_4 = \frac{-21\,|\,00 - 44 \bullet 49 + 46 \bullet 21}{87} = - (38 R\ -16)$$

$$= -38 \ ; \ R_4 = 16$$

49 | –46 | 44 | –38

$$b_5 = \frac{16\,|\,00 + 38 \bullet 49 - 44 \bullet 21}{87} = 29 \ ; \ R_5 = 15$$

49 | –46 | 44 | –38 | 29

Melding the **b**'s and fixing the decimal point results in **B** = 48.54436229 . . . . We can continue the process to additional decimal places if desired. Notice that there is no increase in difficulty for steps after b_2, since **A** has only six digits. Nonetheless, a certain knack has to be acquired to perform the algorithm with any speed.

If the first two digits of **C** are larger than the first two digits of **A**, then $c_1 \mid c_2/a_1$ will produce a three-digit (and therefore inaccurate) quotient. In these cases, we can precede the first digit of **C** with a zero (e.g., **C** = 92472482 becomes 09 | 24 | 72 | 48 | 20). In addition, we should round a_1 to the nearest integer; if **A** were to equal 876221 we would transform **A** into 88 | –38 | 21. Finally, it is again worth mentioning that sometimes division by a particular number can be eased, as in multiplication. For example, $a/15 = 2a/(3 \bullet 10)$, etc.

Since we occasionally encounter the situation where we precede **C** with a zero, perhaps we should add another example where a small number is divided by a four-digit number, say 23/1024 = 0.022460938 . . . . We will add a zero to the end of **C** as well to fill out the two-digit quantity left hanging when the zero is added to the front; we'll sort out the decimal place at the end.

C = 02 | 30

A = 10 | 24

B = C/A = $b_1 \mid b_2 \mid b_3$ . . .

$b_1 = \dfrac{02 \mid 30}{10} = 23$; $R_1 = 0$

23

$b_2 = \dfrac{00 \mid 00 - 23 \bullet 24}{10} = -(55, R\ 2) = -55;\ R_2 = -2$

23 | –55

$b_3 = \dfrac{-2 \mid 00 - (-55) \bullet 24}{10} = 112;\ R_3 = 0$

Since b_3 is three digits long, let $b_2 = -54$ and $R_2 = -12$. Then

$$b_3 = \frac{-12\,|\,00 - (-54) \bullet 24}{10} = 10; \; R_3 = -4$$

$23\,|-54\,|\,10$

$$b_4 = \frac{-4\,|\,00 - 10 \bullet 24}{10} = -64; \; R_4 = 0$$

$23\,|-54\,|\,10\,|-64$

Melding the **b**'s and adjusting the decimal point yields, without too large a total effort, the result $B = 0.022460936\ldots$, and the next step would correct the inaccuracy in the last digit.

While cross division and other methods can be used in calculating a reciprocal exactly, other methods may prove convenient for finding an approximation to the reciprocal of a number near a round number.

For approximate reciprocals of multidigit numbers, we can use an iterative relation for $1/t$ [15]:

$$x_{n+1} = x_n \bullet (2 - tx_n) \tag{2}$$

This relation is derived by assuming that an approximate value x_n is at hand. Then the quantity $(x_n - 1/t)$ is minimized by minimizing $(1 - tx_n)$. Now to ensure that $(1 - tx_{n+1}) < (1 - tx_n)$, we write

$$1 - tx_{n+1} = k(1 - tx_n)^2$$

For **k** = 1, we arrive at Equation 2 by solving this equation for x_{n+1}.

The process is a second-order one, doubling the number of correct digits in each iteration. For $t = (a - b)$, $x_0 = 1/a$, and with (signed) **b** small relative to the round number **a**, we can write the formula for x_1 in a form more suitable for mental calculation:

$$x_1 = x_0 + b/a^2$$

where we can divide **b** by **a** twice rather than by a^2 once to simplify the division. We can take as an example the reciprocal of 387, or 0.00258398 . . . :

$$a = 400$$

$$b = 13$$

$$x_0 = .0025$$

$$x_1 = .0025 + 13/(400)^2$$

$$= .0025 + .0325/400$$

$$= .00258125$$

We would generally not calculate x_2 because of the number of digits in the numbers involved. However, we can get greater accuracy if we choose to use a third-order relation [6],

$$x_{n+1} = x_n + x_n(1 - tx_n) + x_n(1 - tx_n)^2$$

or,

$$x_{n+1} = x_n[1 + (1 - tx_n)(1 + (1 - tx_n))]$$

or, in the earlier notation,

$$x_1 = x_0 + \frac{b + b^2/a}{a^2}$$

Repeating the example above,

$$x_1 = .0025 + \frac{13 + 169/400}{400 \cdot 400}$$

$$= .0025 + \frac{13.4225}{400 \cdot 400}$$

$$= .00258389 \ldots \text{ compared to } .00258398 \ldots$$

Finally, it may be useful at times to convert from a repeating decimal to a fraction. We can limit ourselves to one method as follows. We can see that for a reciprocal $1/t$ yielding a recurring group **g** of period **p**, **t** must divide into $(10^p - 1)$, since it is this remainder of 1 that starts the whole process again. In fact, for the fraction **s/t**,

$$\frac{s}{t} = \frac{g}{10^p - 1}$$

In the chapter on extracting roots, we will see that the lightning calculator A. C. Aitken at least implicitly used this technique. From an initial guess of $50/7 = 7.142286\ldots$ for the square root of 51, he found a closer value of 7.141429. Therefore, he took as a new initial estimate the value $7.141414\ldots$, which he converted into a convenient fraction:

$$7.\overline{14} = 7 + \frac{14}{10^2 - 1} = 707/99$$

The Greatest Common Divisor

It is also occasionally useful to find the greatest common divisor of two numbers **a** and **b**, or gcd(**a,b**). This is especially useful for simplifying the division of a large number by another large number, and it is also utilized in other calculational techniques.

The traditional method of finding the greatest common divisor of two numbers, Euclid's Algorithm, dates from 300 – 400 B.C. [6,7]. The process is iterative and works for any positive integers **a** and **b**. In each step, the larger number is replaced by the remainder when the larger number is divided by the smaller.

As mentioned earlier, we write the relationship between numbers having the same remainder when divided by **b** as $c \equiv a \bmod b$ for **a** > **b**; in the terminology of congruences, **c** is congruent to **a** modulo **b**. When finding the remainder **r** when **a** is divided by **b**, we will use the traditional equals sign (**a** mod **b** = **r**). The reasoning behind Euclid's Algorithm lies in the rules of modular arithmetic, which allow straightforward addition, subtraction and multiplication of terms of this form. For example, since 230/4 leaves a remainder of 2, we write the congruence $2 \equiv 230$ mod 4. By simple modular arithmetic, we can also write that $2 \equiv 200$ mod 4 + 30 mod 4, $2 \equiv 292$ mod $4 - 62$ mod 4, and so forth. Modular multiplication is just as simple; the congruence $2 \equiv 230$ mod 4 can also be expressed as $2 \equiv (10$ mod $4) \times (23$ mod 4). In terms of remainders, we have 230 mod 4 = 2, (200 mod 4 + 30 mod 4) mod 4 = 2, (292 mod $4 - 62$ mod 4) mod 4 = 2, and [(10 mod 4) $\times$ (23 mod 4)] mod 4 = 2. These are easily verified. Remember that if we end up with a negative result, we add 4 until we arrive at a positive number. From above, (292 mod $4 - 62$ mod 4) mod 4 = $(0 - 2)$ mod 4 = -2 mod 4 = 2 mod 4.

Division is more complicated, for if $\mathbf{cd} \equiv \mathbf{ad}$ mod $\mathbf{b}$, then

$$c \equiv a \bmod \frac{b}{\gcd(d,b)}$$

At any rate, to exercise Euclid's Algorithm let us simplify the fraction 2745/13664:

13664 = 4 • 2745 + 2684

2745 = 1 • 2684 + 61

2684 = 44 • 61 + 0

Therefore, gcd(13664,2745) = 61 and we can transform the division to 45/224.

We can modify this procedure by choosing the multiplier of **b** in each step to obtain the minimum absolute value of the remainder. This sometimes gives us a negative remainder, of which the absolute value is used in the next step.

13664 = 5 • 2745 − 61

2745 = 45 • 61 + 0

This is called the least-remainder algorithm for finding the greatest common divisor of two integers [16], and the number of steps is decreased over Euclid's Algorithm by the number of negative remainders that occur.

There is another way of reducing the number of steps and division effort generally required by these algorithms [17]. Notice that we might as well have divided out all multiples of 2 from the even value 13664, since it obviously does not divide 2745. If we do this and start with two odd numbers, we can divide out of the remainder **a** mod **b** in each step all powers of 2 until it is odd. If the remainder is odd to begin with, we can increment the multiplier of **b** to arrive at an even (and now negative) remainder. We find, for our particular example above, that there are savings only in the magnitude of the original numbers since the steps were few due to the fortunate instance of a remainder **a** mod **b** very near **b**. To illustrate,

$$gcd(13664,2745) = gcd(427,2745)$$

$$2745 = 7 \bullet 427 - 4 \bullet 61$$

$$427 = 7 \bullet 61 + 0$$

giving the result $gcd(13664,2745) = 61$. As another example, compare the two methods for finding $gcd(28567,3829) = 7$:

Euclid's Algorithm	Modified Euclid's Algorithm
$28567 = 7 \bullet 3829 + 1764$	$28567 = 7 \bullet 3829 + 4 \bullet 441$
$3829 = 2 \bullet 1764 + 301$	$3829 = 9 \bullet 441 - 4 \bullet 35$
$1764 = 5 \bullet 301 + 259$	$441 = 11 \bullet 35 + 8 \bullet 7$
$301 = 1 \bullet 259 + 42$	$35 = 5 \bullet 7 + 0$
$259 = 6 \bullet 42 + 7$	
$42 = 6 \bullet 7 + 0$	

In general, there is a real savings in doing this. In addition, we can eliminate multiples of other primes from the remainders if these primes are eliminated from the original values **a** and **b**. Again, our first example collapses prior to demonstrating the effect, since extracting, say, a multiplier of the prime number 5 from 2745 leaves 549 and $549 = 1 \bullet 427 + 2 \bullet 61$. However, in the second example we can immediately see that neither 28567 nor 3829 contains a multiple of 5. Therefore, at the second step in the modified Euclid's Algorithm above, we can reduce the already reduced remainder 35 to 7. The operations become

$$28567 = 7 \cdot 3829 + 4 \cdot 441$$

$$3829 = 9 \cdot 441 - 4 \cdot 5 \cdot 7$$

$$441 = 63 \cdot 7 + 0$$

where we now eliminate both the 4 and the 5 in the second line.

If we don't care to perform the division at all to find **a** mod **b**, we can use a method of halving operations throughout. This approach was proposed in 1962 for computer applications [6]. The process involves initially halving **a** or **b** until they are both odd (at least one is assumed odd to begin with or the common factor of 2 is obvious). Then in each step the absolute value of the difference (**a** − **b**) is halved until an odd value results, which then replaces the larger of **a** and **b**.

To return to our earlier example of 2745 and 13664, the even value 13664 is halved until a value of 427 is obtained. Then

$$2745 - 427 = 2318 \rightarrow 1159$$

$$1159 - 427 = 732 \rightarrow 183$$

$$427 - 183 = 244 \rightarrow 61$$

$$183 - 61 = 122 \rightarrow 61$$

$$61 - 61 = 0$$

This algorithm is actually a manifestation of the previous method, with the multiplier in each step being unity and only multiples of 2 being dropped. It is apparent that computers can perform halving operations as simple single machine cycle shifts of binary numbers, so this is a major improvement for them. On the other hand, we are capable of perceiving when higher divisions can be performed, since a number is divisible by 4 if its last two digits are divisible by 4, and by 8 if its last three digits are divisible by 8 (since 4 and 8 divide 100 and 1000, respectively). This significantly decreases our steps in both of the above algorithms. In addition, we can notice that in the fifth step above, 183 is a multiple of 61, so we can terminate the procedure early.

The lowest common multiple (lcm) of two or more numbers can be found from their greatest common divisor. Earlier, we determined that gcd(13664,2745) = 61. The number 61 then contains all prime factors common to both 13664 and 2745. Then 13664 = 61 • 224 and 2745 = 61 • 45, giving lcm(13664,2745) = 61 • 45 • 224. This may be useful for adding and subtracting fractions:

$$\frac{11}{13664} + \frac{7}{2745} = \frac{11 \cdot 45 + 7 \cdot 224}{61 \cdot 45 \cdot 224}$$

$$= \frac{2063}{614880}$$

Error Checking and Divisibility Tests

Error checking of calculations is well worth the little extra effort. A result, of course, should be automatically checked for reasonableness in the overall sense of correct number of digits, reasonable initial digits, and exact last digit.

Other methods generally consist of divisibility tests, and are usually used in addition, subtraction, and multiplication operations. Some divisibility tests provide a remainder if divisibility does not hold, and may be used directly as a division process for one- or two-digit divisors.

Casting out nines, for example, represents a divisibility test for 9, and casting out 99's can improve the accuracy from 89% to 99%. Casting out nines (the nines test), if you recall, amounts to finding the sum of the digits of the number and iterating this process to arrive at a single digit representing the remainder when the number is divided by 9. Intermediate digits like 9 or digits that sum to 9 are easily eliminated during this process. For example,

$$236439 \bmod 9 = (2 + 3 + 6 + 4 + 3 + 9) \bmod 9$$

$$= 27 \bmod 9$$

$$= 0$$

We can also eliminate the "36" combination, since 3 and 6 sum to 9, as well as the lone 9 at the end. The remaining digits (2, 4, and 3) sum to 9, so our answer is 0. We can test the calculation 236439 × 15 = 3546585 as follows:

236439 mod 9 × 15 mod 9 = 3546585 mod 9

0 × 6 = 0   check

Casting out 99's works on digits pairwise from the right. As an example of casting out 99's, consider the calculation 229 × 721 = 165109:

2|29 x 7|21 = 16|51|09

test: 31 • 28 = 76

8|68 = 76

76 = 76   check

The main drawback of the nines test, and one that in practice lowers its accuracy below 89%, is its failure to detect errors in place. That is, if a partial result is shifted an incorrect amount (894 instead of 8940, for example) before being added to the sum being accumulated, it will not be detected in the final result.

A better tack is to cast out elevens, which amounts to subtracting the sum of the even-place digits from the sum of the odd-place digits. If a negative result appears, multiples of 11 are added to bring the overall result to a non-negative integer less than 11.

165109 mod 11 = (9 + 1 + 6) − (0 + 5 + 1) = 10

This elevens test detects errors of place and provides a true 91% accuracy. We can cast out 101's by subtracting the sum of even pairs of digits from the sum of odd pairs of digits, and so forth.

In general, one can construct divisibility tests for various numbers, and these are helpful not only in many division problems, but also for factoring a number whose logarithm is sought. Other than the nines test and elevens test we've mentioned, we have already noted in the last section that a number is divisible by 4 if its last two digits are divisible by 4, and by 8 if its last three digits are divisible by 8, since 4 divides 100 and 8 divides 1000. In addition, we see that a number is divisible by 3 if the result of the nines test is divisible by 3.

One convenient method of testing divisibility by a divisor **d** of a number **N** is to recall a multiple **m** of **d** that lies near a power **t** of ten, the remainder designated here by **r** [2].

$$md = 10^t + r \quad \text{or} \quad 10^t \bmod md = -r$$

If we dissect **N** into **t**-digit groupings n_k,

$$N = n_0 + n_1 10^t + n_2 10^{2t} + n_3 10^{3t} + \ldots$$

$$= n_0 + 10^t(n_1 + 10^t(n_2 + 10^t(n_3 + \ldots)))$$

and therefore,

$$N \bmod md = [n_0 - r(n_1 - r(n_2 - r(n_3 - \ldots)))] \bmod md$$

Simply put, then, one works from the left end of **N**, subtracting each rn_k from n_{k-1}. For the resulting number **R** (consisting of at most **t** digits):

$$R \bmod d = N \bmod d$$

which directly provides us with the remainder if desired. This technique explains why the elevens test works as it does.

For example, to cast out 17's, we know that $6 \cdot 17 = 100 + 2$. Therefore, **r** = 2 and since $100 = 10^2$, we separate **N** into pairs of digits. Beginning on the left, we subtract twice the digit pair from the next pair, dropping multiples of 17 from any pair when convenient. For **N** = 165109,

$$16|51|09 \rightarrow 19|09 \rightarrow 2|09 \rightarrow 5$$

and 165109 leaves a remainder 5 when divided by 17. As an aside, we've also found here that 165109 mod 6 = 5 as well.

There are a number of convenient divisors. For example, division by the prime number 37 is eased because $37 \cdot 27 = 1000 - 1$. In addition, since each group can be reduced by any multiple of the divisor, and $3 \cdot 37 = 111$, we can easily subtract multiples of 111 from each triplet:

$$784,165,109 \rightarrow 7,54,-2 \rightarrow 61,-2 \rightarrow 59 \rightarrow 22$$

Another one of interest is $7 \cdot 11 \cdot 13 = 1001$, useful for simplifying the tests for any or all of these factors:

$$1,109,185 \rightarrow 108,185 \rightarrow 77$$

Therefore, 1109185 is divisible by 7 and 11 and leaves a remainder of 12 when divided by 13.

We can use a related algorithm [18–20] for determining the divisibility of a number N by an odd integer d whose last digit is not a 5. A disadvantage of this method is that, except for $d = 3$ or 9, the remainder N mod d does not emerge if nonzero. However, the method is interesting and can be useful.

The basic approach for a number N consisting of a sequence of digits is to add a multiple m of the terminal digit to the number formed by the remaining digits. This process is iterated, and each resulting number N_1, N_2, N_3, etc. is divisible by d if the original number N is. We terminate the process when we easily see whether or not a value of N is indeed divisible by d.

We consider a divisor d consisting of digits $D_1 d_2$, where d_2 is a single digit and D_1 can be multidigit or single-digit, including 0. The multiplier m is given for $d_2 = 1$ as $(-D_1)$ and for $d_2 = 9$ as $(D_1 + 1)$. The absolute value of m here represents the multiple of 10 that N is either one greater than or one less than; the negative sign for $d_2 = 1$ corresponds to the alternating signs in the elevens test. For $d_2 = 3$ or 7, we multiply d by 3 and arrive at one of the cases above.

For example, the number $N = 304$ can be tested for divisibility by $d = 19$ as follows:

$$N = 304$$

$$N_1 = 30 + 2 \cdot 4 = 38$$

$$N_2 = 3 + 2 \cdot 8 = 19$$

Therefore, 304 is divisible by 19. For $d_2 = 9$ without multiplication by 3, the process will always terminate in d if d divides N. In fact, for the number c constructed of final digits of all but this last N, the quotient q is given by $(10^t - c)$, where t is one less than the number of digits in N. Here, $q = 100 - 84 = 16$, so $304 = 19 \cdot 16$.

For $d_2 = 1$ without multiplication by 3, the process will always terminate in zero if d divides N, and then $q = c$. As an example,

$$N = 83049 \qquad d = 31$$

$$N_1 = 8304 - 3 \cdot 9 = 8277$$

$$N_2 = 827 - 3 \cdot 7 = 806$$

$$N_3 = 80 - 3 \cdot 6 = 62$$

$$N_4 = 6 - 3 \cdot 2 = 0$$

and

$$q = 2679$$

When d_2 becomes 9 or 1 upon multiplying d by 3, the process will end with a multiple of d if d divides N. Extraction of the quotient is not straightforward. As examples, consider

$d = 13$, becoming 39	$d = 27$, becoming 81
$N = 15587$	$N = 2619$
$N_1 = 1558 + 4 \cdot 7 = 1586$	$N_1 = 261 - 8 \cdot 9 = 189$
$N_2 = 158 + 4 \cdot 6 = 182$	$N_2 = 18 - 8 \cdot 9 = -54$,
$N_3 = 18 + 4 \cdot 2 = 26$,	divisible by 27
divisible by 13	

An extension of this strategy consists of adding or subtracting a multiple of a *group* of terminal digits of N. While in most cases this is too cumbersome to be of much practical use for mental work, a few cases may be useful [20,21]. For example, divisibility of N by $d = 29$ or 23 can be determined by subtracting twice the number formed by the last three digits of N from the number formed by the remaining digits, and then iterating. For $N = 5851417$,

$N_1 = 5851 - 2 \cdot 417 = 5017$

$N_2 = 5 - 2 \cdot 17 = -29$

which shows divisibility by 29, but not 23. The quotient is hidden.

The source of this technique, as you probably have guessed by now, lies in the fact that 2001 is divisible by 23 and 29. Based on this principle, Smith [3] lists the methods lightning calculator Wim Klein might use to determine possible factors of the number **N** = 114043 (note that these methods don't directly provide correct remainders if nonzero). In each case shown in Table 1 the reduced number (and therefore **N**) is not divisible by the divisors.

We can also use Euclid's Algorithm or its modifications to test divisibility of a number by several primes at once [7,9]. Euclid's Algorithm provides the greatest common divisor of two given numbers. If one of these is the number **N** to be tested and the other is a product of some prime numbers, the greatest common divisor will be divisible by any of these primes that divide **N**.

This method may be used with a large product of primes, say up to $N^{1/2}$. The intermediate remainders of Euclid's Algorithm collapse rapidly, but the initial division is an extreme one. We

Table 1
Some Divisibility Tests (N = 114043) [3]

Divisors	Reduction	Reason
7, 11, 13	$114 - 043 = 71$	$7 \times 11 \times 13 = 1001$
37	$114 + 043 = 157$	$37 \times 27 = 999$
23, 29	$114 - 2(043) = 28$	$23 \times 29 \times 3 = 2001$
31, 43	$114 + 4(043) = 286$	$31 \times 43 \times 3 = 3999$
19	$1140 + 4(43) = 1312$	$19 \times 21 = 399$
17, 47	$1140 + 8(43) = 1484$	$17 \times 47 = 799$
41	$1140 + 16(43) = 1828$	$41 \times 39 = 1599$
67	$1140 - 2(43) = 1054$	$67 \times 3 = 201$
89	$114 - 8(43) = 796$	$89 \times 9 = 801$
53	$1140 - 9(43) = 753$	$53 \times 17 = 901$

will consider here a less ambitious example to demonstrate its possible use in mental calculation.

First, examine those primes that have been treated so far in this section. Working up through the two-digit primes, we have derived perhaps the most efficient divisibility tests for the numbers 3, 5, 7, 11, 13, 17, 19, 23, 29, 31, 37, 41, 43, and those of the form $(10m + 1)$ and $(10m - 1)$ above this. Therefore, let us consider the product 141987 of the primes 47, 53, and 57. This number is located near enough to 142000 to ease our calculations. We will test the number $N = 760603$ for divisibility by these primes using what we called the modified Euclidean Algorithm. We discard easy small prime factors we know are not divisors, such as 2 and 5, from convenient positive or negative remainders in each step.

$$760603 = 5 \bullet 142000 + 50603$$

$$= 5 \bullet 141987 + 4 \bullet 12667$$

$$141987 = 11 \bullet 12667 + 2 \bullet (5)^2 \bullet 53$$

$$12667 = 239 \bullet 53 + 0$$

Therefore, 760603 is divisible by 53, but not by 47 or 57. The advantage over long division by each prime increases with the size of N and the number of primes included in the product, within the capabilities we possess.

Of course, N can be smaller than the product of the primes. For $N = 26269$ we have

$$141987 = 5 \bullet 26269 + 2 \bullet 5321$$

$$26269 = 5 \bullet 5321 - (2)^4 \bullet 21$$

We can stop here since 21 is less than 47, and we conclude that 26269 is not divisible by 47, 53, or 57.

The general procedures of nines tests and elevens tests can be adapted to other bases. It is occasionally useful, though I have not seen it presented or practiced by anyone else, to check a hexadecimal equivalent by casting out 17's. For the hexadecimal base,

base 16, this is exactly equivalent to casting out elevens in the decimal base:

$$F29D \rightarrow (D + 2) - (9 + F) \rightarrow 15 - 24 \rightarrow -9 \rightarrow 8$$

$$62109 \rightarrow 6 \mid 21 \mid 09 \rightarrow 9 \mid 09 \rightarrow -9 \rightarrow 8$$

This leads naturally to the question of possible benefits of changing bases [9]. Whenever two divisors can be expressed as $(b + 1)$ and $(b - 1)$, we can convert the given number to the base **b** and cast out nines and elevens. For example, to determine if **N** = 13949 is divisible by 29 or 31, we can convert to base 30:

$$13949/30 = 464 \text{ remainder } 29$$

$$464/30 = 15 \quad \text{remainder } 14$$

$$15/30 = 0 \quad \text{remainder } 15$$

Then $(15 + 14 + 29) = 58$, revealing a factor of 29, and $(15 + 29 - 14) = 30$, eliminating the factor 31.

Converting bases can be awkward when they are not multiples of powers of 10. However, we can choose a convenient base that, when increased or decreased by one, is a multiple of the divisors we are testing. Taylor [9] gives base 50 as such a base for divisors 3, 7, and 17, as $49 = (7)^2$ and $51 = 17 \bullet 3$.

Other bases can provide for four divisors less than 100 at once, including 300 (since 13 and 23 divide 299 and 7 and 43 divide 301), 900 (for 29, 31, 17, and 53) and as we have seen before, 1000 (for 37, 7, 11, and 13). Taylor gives a table like Table 2 of convenient bases for divisors less than 100, including all primes except 73, 83, and 97. The prime numbers 3 and 9 actually may appear in a number of cases here, but are shown in their most useful base of 10.

Actually, we did something reminiscent of this in our earlier method for **d** ending in a 1, 3, 7, or 9. If we regroup the net operations in, say, our earlier example of **N** = 304 and **d** = 19, we find

$$3 \bullet 1 + 0 \bullet 2 + 4 \bullet (2)^2 = 19$$

Table 2
Convenient Bases for Divisibility Tests

Base	Nines Test Factors	Elevens Test Factors
10	9,3	11
20	19	21,7
30	29	31
40	39,13	41
50	49,7	51,17
60	59	61
70	69,23	71
80	79	81
90	89	91,7,13
100	99,11	—
110	—	37
200	—	67
300	13,23	7,43
800	17,47	89
900	29,31	17,53
1000	37	7,11,13

and for $N = 51243$ and $d = 31$,

$$5 \bullet 1 - 1 \bullet 3 + 2 \bullet 9 - 4 \bullet 27 + 3 \bullet 81 = 155$$

$$1 \bullet 1 - 5 \bullet 3 + 5 \bullet 9 = 31$$

Factorization

Finding factors of integers is often useful in simplifying, for example, multiplications of medium-sized numbers. However, for large numbers it is surprising in its difficulty; the relative problem of factoring large integers compared to multiplying them is exploited in certain forms of cryptography nicely described by Riesel [7] and Eynden [22].

The fundamental theorem of arithmetic states that any factorable, or composite, integer can be represented in one and only one way (barring ones and simple re-orderings) as a product of positive prime numbers. Recall that a prime number, or prime, is a positive integer other than 1 that is divisible only by itself and 1. These include the numbers 2, 3, 5, 7, 11, 13, 17, and so forth. In this section and the next we will examine processes that find factors of integers and that lend themselves to mental solution. In fact, we will explore this area well beyond its useful scope because this represents a fascinating topic for mental recreation and challenge.

To begin, we can apply our earlier divisibility tests for small primes. On the other hand, "Even though a random number **n** usually has small factors (since **n** is divisible by 2 with probability 1/2, by 3 with probability 1/3, by 5 with probability 1/5, etc.) it is very unusual for **n** to have *only* small factors." [6]

Riesel [7] remarks that large integers very rarely have many prime factors, despite popular perceptions. Moreover, the largest prime factor of **N** would have approximately 62% of the number of digits of **N**. As a cautionary note, the integers in the range we work in (or particular ones chosen, of course) may have significantly different characteristics from these.

To continue, what techniques can we put to bear other than divisibility tests? One convenient and interesting method (the first systematic one, in fact) was developed and used by the mathematician Pierre de Fermat (1601–1665) and will find the largest factor (prime or not) of **N**, obviously not greater than $N^{1/2}$. It also has the capability, amazingly enough, of eliminating division entirely [6,7,9,10,23–25].

First, assuming our number **N** is odd (the non-trivial case), we can locate the midpoint of any two factors, which will both be odd, and call this integer **x**. Then for $y < x$,

$$(x - y) \bullet (x + y) = N$$

$$x^2 - y^2 = N$$

or

$$x^2 - N = y^2 \tag{3}$$

Therefore, we must find integers **x** and **y** satisfying Equation 3. We first set x_0 equal to the lowest value it can be, i.e., the nearest integer above $N^{1/2}$, and increment x in a series of steps. Since $[(x + 1)^2 - N] = (x^2 - N) + (2x + 1)$, we increase each $(x^2 - N)$ value by $(2x + 1)$, or by the previous increase plus 2. When we find that $(x^2 - N)$ is the perfect square of an integer y, we extract $(x - y)$ and $(x + y)$ as factors of N. Obviously, the nearer the average of the factors is to $N^{1/2}$, or correspondingly the nearer the factors are to each other, the closer the successful x will be to x_0. In fact, to find the factor $a = kN^{1/2}$, where $0 < k < 1$, we require $(1 - k)N^{1/2}/2k$ steps, which can be large for small k.

To illustrate this algorithm, we can take $N = 1403$:

x	$x^2 - N$
38	41
39	41 + 77 = 118
40	197
41	278
42	361

Since $361 = (19)^2$, then $1403 = 23 \bullet 61$, because $42 - 19 = 23$ and $42 + 19 = 61$.

The task of determining whether a perfect square has emerged is made much easier by realizing that such a number must have its last two digits as 00, e1, e4, 25, d6, or e9, where e is an even digit and d is an odd digit. In the example above, only 41 and 361 meet this criterion.

Actually, we can extend these rules. A square ending in 25 can only end in 125, 225, or 625. Also, numbers ending in e1 and e9 can only have an even thousands digit if 4 divides e. Endings of this sort are:

e01	e09
d21	d29
e41	e49
d61	d69
e81	e89

Implicit in this, since divisibility by 4 is determined by the last two digits only, is the fact that a number of the form $(4k - 1)$ can never be a square; squares can only be of the form $4k$ or $(8k + 1)$ [10].

These enhancements do not help us in distinguishing 41 and 361 as squares if we didn't know.

In general, we can easily construct a table of values of x^2 mod m (called the quadratic residues of m) which can help; these are given for $m = 3$ to 9 as the third column in Table 3. For example, x^2 mod 9 must leave a residue of 0, 1, 4, or 7, a nines test that is passed here by 361 but not 41. Riesel notes that x^2 mod 16 gives 0, 1, 4, or 9 as residues, a test almost twice as efficient. While it is very nice for computers to work in this base, it is also a nice rule for us. Both numbers pass this sieve as well!

There is another means of simplifying the entire process using modular arithmetic. Since 1403 = 2 mod 3 and for any x, x^2 mod $3 = 0$ or 1, then $(x^2 - N)$ mod $3 = 1$ or 2, respectively. Again, for any y, y^2 mod $3 = 0$ or 1, so for $(x^2 - N) = y^2$, then x^2 mod $3 = 0$, giving x mod $3 = 0$. For $N = 2$ mod 3, then, we need only consider values of x that are multiples of 3 by the use of this sieve. From $x = 39$ we can therefore jump directly to $x = 42$, increasing $(x^2 - N)$ by $3(39 + 42) = 243$.

We can construct a table of possible values of x mod m for various m. The completed table for some representative values of m is given in Table 3.

In this table, even values of N mod m do not occur for even m because multiples of an even number are even and N is odd. However, multiples of odd numbers can be even, so both even and odd values of N mod m can occur for odd m.

Looking at Table 3, we note that entries for N mod $6 = 3$ and N mod $9 = 3,6$ do not exist since N mod $3 = 0$ in this case. Also, we observe that the cases $m = 3$ and 6 are redundant to the case $m = 9$, and the case $m = 4$ is redundant to that of $m = 8$. In addition, the cases $m = 8$ and 9 have relatively few x^2 mod m values for their size, and the results for $m = 9$ are easily remembered. In fact, the sums of the possible x mod m values in every row of every m, as well as the sums of $(x^2 - N)$ mod m values, are intriguing in themselves.

In summary, perhaps we can best approach the solution to a factoring problem as follows:

Table 3
Modular Sieves for Fermat's Method of Factoring

m	x mod m	x² mod m	N mod m	(x² − N) mod m	Possible x mod m
3	0,1,2	0,1,1	1	2,0,0	1,2 (not a mult. of 3)
			2	1,2,2	0 (mult. of 3)
4	0,1,2,3	0,1,0,1	1	3,0,3,0	1,3 (odd)
			3	1,2,1,2	0,2, (even)
5	0,1,2, 3,4	0,1,4,4,1	1	4,0,3,3,0	0,1,4
			2	3,4,2,2,4	1,4
			3	2,3,1,1,3	2,3
			4	1,2,0,0,2	0,2,3
6	0,1,2, 3,4,5	0,1,4,3,4,1	1	5,0,3,2,3,0	1,2,4,5 (not a mult. of 3)
			5	1,2,5,4,5,2	0,3 (mult. of 3)
7	0,1,2,3, 4,5,6	0,1,4,2, 2,4,1	1	6,0,3,1, 1,3,0	1,3,4,6
			2	5,6,2,0, 0,2,6	2,3,4,5
			3	4,5,1,6, 6,1,5	0,2,5
			4	3,4,0,5, 5,0,4	1,2,5,6
			5	2,3,6,4, 4,6,3	0,3,4
			6	1,2,5,3, 3,5,2	0,1,6

(table continued on next page)

Table 3
Continued

m	x mod m	x^2 mod m	N mod m	$(x^2 - N)$ mod m	Possible x mod m
8	0,1,2,3, 4,5,6,7	0,1,4,1, 0,1,4,1	1	7,0,3,0, 7,0,3,0	1,3,5,7 (odd)
			3	5,6,1,6, 5,6,1,6	2,6 (two + mult. of 4)
			5	3,4,7,4, 3,4,7,4	1,3,5,7 (odd)
			7	1,2,5,2, 1,2,5,2	0,4 (mult. of 4)
9	0,1,2,3, 4,5,6,7,8	0,1,4,0, 7,7,0,4,1	1	8,0,3,8, 6,6,8,3,0	1,8
			2	7,8,2,7, 5,5,7,2,8	0,3,6 (mult. of 3)
			4	5,6,0,5, 3,3,5,0,6	2,7
			5	4,5,8,4, 2,2,4,8,5	0,3,6 (mult. of 3)
			7	2,3,6,2, 0,0,2,6,3	4,5
			8	1,2,5,1, 8,8,1,5,2	0,3,6 (mult. of 3)

1. Check for divisibility by 2, 3, 5, 7, and 11 using standard divisibility tests.
2. Find x_0 as the nearest integer larger than $N^{1/2}$. Estimate the range required of **x**; since $11 < (x - y) \leq 13$, a conveniently calculated upper limit on **x** is $(N/25) + 6$.
3. Find **N** mod 9 (by the nines test) to reduce possibilities of **x**. Find **N** mod 8 to further reduce them. Optionally, find **N** mod 5 and **N** mod 7.

4. Try possible **x**'s greater than x_0, checking the two-digit endings of $(x^2 - N)$ for possible squares. For cases that pass this sieve as well, determine if $y = (x^2 - N)^{1/2}$ is an integer. If so, $(x - y) \cdot (x + y) = N$.

This is actually much easier and more powerful than it appears. In our earlier example of $N = 1403$, which appears trivial now, N mod 9 = 8 implies that x mod 3 = 0. Also, N mod 8 = 3 (remember to look only at the last three digits) and therefore x mod 4 = 2. The latter two conditions, incidentally, amount to requiring x to be an odd multiple of 6. In the total range of x from 38 to 62, only $x = 42$ and $x = 54$ are possible, and $[(52)^2 - N]$ does not clear the two-digit ending sieve. The result $x = 42$, $y = 19$ is therefore easily obtained.

If we had memorized or reconstructed the rules for $m = 5$, we could have found that x mod 5 = 2 or 3. Then $x = 42$ is the only candidate, the next possible value, 78, being beyond the range of x. For $m = 7$, if we bothered to recall it, we would find x mod 7 = 0, 2, or 5, and the next possible value after $x = 42$ would be 114.

As mentioned, Fermat's "difference of squares" method of factoring works from y small toward y large, so two factors a and b far from each other will take a long time to locate. If it seems that we are not having any luck, we can try multiplying N by a factor k. For odd k, we will find the factors a and kb quickly if a is approximately equal to kb. The case of even k's is a little complicated, for then kN will be even. For $k = 2$, kN cannot have a midpoint of two factors. If we multiply x and y by 2, then $(2x - 2y) \cdot (2x + 2y)$ is a valid factorization, giving $k = 4$, but the factors are the same relative distance apart. For $k = 8$, we then have the valid factorization $(4x - 4y) \cdot (2x + 2y)$, giving a fast solution for a approximately equal to $2b$. In general, any even value of k should be a multiple of 8 when a is an even multiple of b. A case where a/b is approximately $3/2$, of course, would benefit from setting $k = 6$, the case a/b approximately $5/3$ by letting $k = 15$, and so forth.

Given that we generally have no feel for the relative sizes of the factors, we can abandon the factoring process after a while and try multiplying by a new factor. Riesel [7] suggests multiplying by a composite k containing various small divisors (such as 24). There is a legendary feat of factorization by Fermat, often quoted as requiring a primality test lost in history, wherein the number $N = 100895598169$ was reduced to 112303×898423. It turns out that $8N = (898424)^2 - 898424 = 898424(898424 - 1) = 8 \times 112303 \times 898423$.

There are situations where we can eliminate most values of x in Fermat's method without constructing or recalling the modular sieves we have developed. While this falls very near the domain of properties of particular numbers, it is of such great potential that I feel it is worth discussing.

It is known [7] from A. M. Legendre (1752–1833) that odd integers N of the form $N = a^n + b^n$ for any integer n and of the form $N = a^n - b^n$ for any odd n, where $\gcd(a,b) = 1$, have prime factors of the form $p = 2kn + 1$, excluding prime divisors of algebraic factors of N of the form $(a^m \pm b^m)$ for $m < n$. Of course, for $N = a^n - b^n$ for n even, we already have factors as $(a^{n/2} \pm b^{n/2})$.

We will discuss the clause concerning algebraic factors in a moment. In general, this sieve may appear to limit possible values of x in Fermat's method to $1/n$ of their number otherwise, but it actually limits them to $1/(2n^2)$, a significant advantage. In fact, we need only consider values of x for which

$$x \equiv \frac{N + 1}{2} \bmod (2n^2)$$

The occasional number of the given forms $(a^n \pm b^n)$ benefit greatly from this sieve. There are more of them around than you might expect, particularly since b can be as small as 1.

As an example, consider $N = 1027 = (10)^3 + (3)^3$. Then $x \equiv 514 \bmod 18 \equiv 10 \bmod 18$. Since our values of x would normally begin at 33, we can now jump directly to $x = 46$ and begin incrementing by 18:

x	$x^2 - N$
46	1089

We find $1089 = (33)^2$ immediately, so $1027 = 13 \cdot 79$.

Now we return to the matter of algebraic factors. These are factors of algebraic expressions, such as $3xy + 2y - 3x - 2 =$

$(3\mathbf{x} + 2) \bullet (\mathbf{y} - 1)$. Of course, if $\mathbf{N}$ can be expressed as a factorable polynomial, we immediately have two factors. Now, since

$$a^2 - b^2 = (a + b) \bullet (a - b)$$

$$a^3 - b^3 = (a - b) \bullet (a^2 + ab + b^2)$$

$$a^4 - b^4 = (a^2 + b^2) \bullet (a^2 - b^2)$$

$$= (a^2 + b^2) \bullet (a + b) \bullet (a - b)$$

$$a^5 - b^5 = (a - b) \bullet (a^4 + a^3b + a^2b^2 + ab^3 + b^4)$$

and

$$a^2 + b^2 \text{ is unfactorable}$$

$$a^3 + b^3 = (a + b) \bullet (a^2 - ab + b^2)$$

$$a^4 + b^4 \text{ is unfactorable}$$

$$a^5 + b^5 = (a + b) \bullet (a^4 - a^3b - a^2b^2 - ab^3 + b^4)$$

then most of the expressions $(a^n + b^n)$ or $(a^n - b^n)$ reveal two factors immediately. The factor $(a + b)$ is associated with the expression $(a^n + b^n)$, and the factor $(a - b)$ with the expression $(a^n - b^n)$. Therefore, we could instantly have known earlier that one of the factors of $1027 = (10)^3 + (3)^3$ is $(10 + 3)$.

Legendre's theorem is powerful because it defines a sieve for *all* prime factors other than those dividing these algebraic factors of the form $(a^n \pm b^n)$, and as we discussed, most numbers contain a variety of prime factors. Riesel cautions us to test if prime factors derived from algebraic factors are multiple factors before we search for those of the form $(2\mathbf{k}n + 1)$.

Let us examine a trivial case, $\mathbf{N} = 1001 = (10)^3 + 1$. We immediately know that $(10 + 1) = 11$ is one factor, and it accordingly is not of the form $(6\mathbf{k} + 1)$. The only algebraic factor of this type is $(a + b)$, and no other prime divides it. Dividing $\mathbf{N}$ by 11, we find the cofactor $\mathbf{N}' = 91$ (which is not divisible by 11 again) and we know its prime factors now to be of the form

(6k + 1). We can test **k** = 1, 2, 3, etc., finding 7 and 13 or, more generally, we can use Fermat's method with **x** ≡ 46 mod 18 ≡ 10 mod 18. Then we find that $(10)^2 - 91 = (3)^2$, giving us the remaining prime factors 7 and 13.

Considering a less trivial case, let **N** = 2581 = $(50)^2 + (9)^2$. There are no algebraic factors here, so all prime factors are of the form (4**k** + 1). Using Fermat's method, we know then that **x** ≡ 1291 mod 8 ≡ 3 mod 8. We would normally begin this method with **x** = 51, and since 51 mod 8 = 3, we persist, increasing **x** in each step by 8:

x	$x^2 - N$
51	20
59	900 = $(30)^2$

Therefore, 2581 = (59 − 30) • (59 + 30) = 29 • 89. If as recommended earlier we had memorized the modular sieve from Table 3 for **m** = 9, then the result **N** mod 9 = 7 would imply that **x** mod 9 = 4 or 5, catapulting us immediately to **x** = 59 as our initial value.

There is a variation of Fermat's method called, by Vaes, the method of remainders [10]. Setting **y** = (**N** − 1)/2 and **x** = (**N** + 1)/2, giving **N** = $x^2 - y^2$, then a remainder **r** obtained by dividing **y** by **p** will give a remainder (**r** + 1) when **x** is divided by **p**. Therefore, if we divide **y** by **p** and find **r**, and (2**r** + 1) is divisible by **p**, then **N** is divisible by **p**.

For example, for our earlier **N** = 1403, we divide (**N** − 1) by 2 (an immediate advantage) to arrive at **y** = 701. Then we begin with Equation 1 to rewrite the value of **y** in each step, producing various remainders **r**. We have

$$y = (26)^2 + 25$$

$$= 25 • 27 + 26$$

$$= 24 • 28 + 29$$

$$= 23 • 29 + 34$$

etc.

and we continue, where the remainder **r** is the last number in each step, until $(2r + 1)$ is a multiple of one of the multiplied terms in that step. In the last step shown, $2 \bullet 34 + 1 = 69$, a multiple of 23, so 23 is a factor of 1403. Perhaps finding whether a number is divisible by another is easier than finding if it is a square, but the memory requirements are greater at each step. We can ease the task if, instead of adding the squares of 1, 2, 3, and so forth to our original remainder in each step, we simply add the odd numbers 1, 3, 5, 7 to the remainder in the previous step or, better yet, add twice the odd integers cumulatively to our original $(2r_0 + 1)$ value:

$r_0 = 25$

$2r_0 + 1 = 51$

$2r_1 + 1 = 51 + 2 \bullet 1 = 53$

$2r_2 + 1 = 53 + 2 \bullet 3 = 59$

$2r_3 + 1 = 59 + 2 \bullet 5 = 69$

etc.

In a different vein, we can use triangular numbers instead of squares in Fermat's algorithm [9,10]. Triangular numbers represent the total number of items in the rows of a triangular array up through the tth row, such as in the pin arrangement in bowling. The triangular numbers are given, then, as 1, 3, 6, 10, 15, 21, etc. and are given by the expression

$$t_x = \frac{x(x + 1)}{2} \qquad x = 1, 2, 3, \ldots$$

Now, since

$$\frac{x(x + 1)}{2} - \frac{y(y + 1)}{2} = \frac{(x - y) \bullet (x + y + 1)}{2} = N$$

or

$$t_x - N = t_y$$

then if we find a triangular number t_x that after subtraction of N results in another triangular number t_y, we have factored N. The denominator 2 in the factored expression for N divides whichever term in the numerator comes out even.

As we did with squares, we begin with the nearest t_x above N; x is found here by extracting the square root of $2N$. Since

$$\frac{x(x + 1)}{2} = \frac{(x - 1)(x - 1 + 1)}{2} + x$$

or

$$t_x = t_{x-1} + x$$

we can increase the previous value $(t_{x-1} - N)$ by x in each step. Of course we knew that, since we form consecutive triangular numbers by adding another row in the bowling pin arrangement and the xth row contains x pins. Therefore, we do not have to keep track of our value of x as we proceed. In our earlier example of $N = 1403$, we have

$(2806)^{1/2}$ is approximately 53

$(53 \bullet 54)/2 = 1431$

x	$t_x - N$
53	28

and we collapse immediately as $28 = (7 \bullet 8)/2 = t_7$. The factors of 1403 are then $(53 - 7)/2 = 23$ and $(53 + 7 + 1) = 61$. We seem to bear out Taylor's claim that the great advantage of using triangular numbers over squares lies in the reduction in the number of steps involved. Experimenting with various numbers reveals the startling truth of this for factors not exceedingly close to one another.

Let's try factoring another number to show the values added in each step:

N = 21449

$(2N)^{1/2}$ is approximately 207

$$\frac{207 \cdot 208}{2} = \frac{200 \cdot 215 + 56}{2} = 21528$$

x (or adder)	$t_x - N$
207	79
208	79 + 208 = 287
209	287 + 209 = 496

but 496 = (31 • 32)/2. Then the factors are (209 − 31)/2 = 89 and (209 + 31 + 1) = 241, showing an amazing convergence to a solution with such widely differing factors.

How do we determine if a number is triangular? Triangular numbers end in the digits 0, 1, 03, 53, 5, 6, 28, or 78, and the first such number in the last example is 496. The single-digit endings listed here can be preceded by any digit, so we unfortunately end up with 44 possible two-digit endings instead of the 22 we had for squares. Now t_x mod 9 = 0, 1, 3, or 6, a test easily performed by casting out nines. Since 496 passes this sieve as well, we can explicitly check it by finding $(2 \cdot 496)^{1/2}$ as approximately 31. Then we find that 2(496) = $(31)^2$ + 31, or equivalently that 2 • 496 = 31 • 32, and we are done.

We can construct a table, as for Fermat's method, of possible values of **x** mod **m** for various moduli **m**. This is given in Table 4 for various moduli.

Again, even values of **N** mod **m** will not occur for even **m**, as **N** is odd and multiples of an even number are even. We also eliminated **N** mod 6 = 3 and **N** mod 9 = 3 and 6, as these would then be divisible by 3, a prime factor considered to have been tried already.

Overall, we are not as fortunate here as we were for Fermat's method. The cases **m** = 3 and 6 are again redundant to the case **m** = 9, and perhaps in general the most efficient procedure is to simply memorize the case **m** = 9, which is not difficult. In our previous example, 21449 = 2 mod 9, so **x** = 2 or 6 mod 9. The first such **x** ≥ 207 is 209, and the next occurs at 213. To jump from 209 to 213 we would have added 4 • 211.5 = 846 to arrive at 1342.

Table 4
Modular Sieves for the Triangular
Number Method of Factoring

m	x mod m	t_x mod m	N mod m	$(t_x - N)$ mod m	Possible x mod m
3	0,1,2	0,1,0	1	2,0,2	1
			2	1,2,1	0,2
4	0,1,2,3	0,1,3,0	1	3,0,2,3	0,1,3
			3	1,2,0,1	1,2,3 (not a mult. of 4)
5	0,1,2, 3,4	0,1,3,1,0	1	4,0,2,0,4	1,3
			2	3,4,1,4,3	0,2,4
			3	2,3,0,3,2	1,2,3
			4	1,2,4,2,1	0,4
6	0,1,2, 3,4,5	0,1,3,0,4,0	1	5,0,2,5,3,5	1,4
			5	1,2,4,1,5,1	0,2,3,5
7	0,1,2,3, 4,5,6	0,1,3,6, 3,1,0	1	6,0,2,5, 2,0,6	0,1,5,6
			2	5,6,1,4, 1,6,5	1,2,4,5
			3	4,5,0,3, 0,5,4	2,3,4
			4	3,4,6,2, 6,4,3	0,2,4,6
			5	2,3,5,1, 5,3,2	1,3,5
			6	1,2,4,0, 4,2,1	0,3,6

Table 4
Continued

m	x mod m	t_x mod m	N mod m	$(t_x - N)$ mod m	Possible x mod m
8	0,1,2,3, 4,5,6,7	0,1,3,6, 2,7,5,0	1	7,0,2,5, 1,6,4,7	0,1,2,3, 4,5,7
			3	5,6,0,3, 7,4,2,5	0,1,2,3, 4,6,7
			5	3,4,6,1, 5,2,0,3	0,2,3,4, 5,6,7
			7	1,2,4,7, 3,0,6,1	0,1,2,4, 5,6,7
9	0,1,2,3, 4,5,6,7,8	0,1,3,6, 1,6,3,1,0	1	8,0,2,5, 0,5,2,0,8	1,4,7
			2	7,8,1,4, 8,4,1,8,7	2,6
			4	5,6,8,2, 6,2,8,6,5	1,4,7
			5	4,5,7,1, 5,1,7,5,4	3,5
			7	2,3,5,8, 3,8,5,3,2	1,4,7
			8	1,2,4,7, 2,7,4,2,1	0,8

There is another method of factorization for numbers of the form $(4k + 1)$, where k is a positive integer. It has been proven that a prime number of this form (i.e., 1 mod 4) can be expressed as the sum of squares $(a^2 + b^2)$, with $gcd(a,b) = 1$, in one and only one way; otherwise, the number is composite. Fermat first discovered this relationship which was proved a hundred years later by Euler. Fermat called this fact "the fundamental theorem on right-angled triangles," as for a prime **p** there is only one such figure with integral sides and a hypotenuse equal to $p^{1/2}$. The method of factoring when there are two sums of squares is termed Euler's method, although it was given much earlier by Frénicle and Mersenne [23].

I mention this technique largely because of its use by at least two lightning calculators in this century [3]. In my opinion, its main disadvantages are that it can be used on only half of all odd numbers, it requires checking every possible sum of squares (albeit sieved), and it requires subsequent extraction of the factors from the squares if the number is composite and has at least two such sums.

There are two basic methods for finding pairs of squares that add to a number **N**, which we term for two sets of squares

$$N = a^2 + b^2 = c^2 + d^2$$

The first method parallels Fermat's method of factoring, where we now find whether $(N - x^2)$ is a square rather than our previous quantity $(x^2 - N)$. We can test every value **a** between $N^{1/2}$ and $(N/2)^{1/2}$, or $0.7N^{1/2}$, at which point we begin duplication with **x** and **y** interchanging roles. In analogy with Fermat's method, we begin with **x** just less than $N^{1/2}$ and decrease **x** as we proceed. We need only add $(2x + 1)$ in each step, or simply increase the adder in the previous step by 2:

$$N - x^2 = N - (x + 1)^2 + 2x + 1$$

The two-digit endings for squares can be used with advantage here.

Let us take the example **N** = 1433, which is of the type allowed since 33 = 1 mod 4.

x	$N - x^2$
37	64
36	137 = 64 + 73
35	208 = 137 + 71
34	277
33	344
32	409
31	472
30	533
29	592
28	649
27	704
26	757

We stop because 757 is larger than ($N/2$). We see as we mentally trace these steps that there is one and only one sum of two relatively prime (gcd(a,b) = 1) squares that add to 1433, $(37)^2 + (8)^2 = 1433$, revealing that 1433 is prime.

Let's try N = 1457:

x	$N - x^2$
38	13
37	88
36	161
35	232
34	301
33	368
32	433
31	496
30	557
29	616
28	673
27	728

and we find that 1457 is composite, but we have no sum of squares to extract factors. Actually, this situation will occur whenever any prime factor of N is of the form ($4n + 3$) and is of an odd power; here, 1457 = 31 • 47 and both factors are of this form [26]. Fortunately, this is not always the case. For N = 1537, we have

x	$N - x^2$
39	16
38	93
37	168
36	241
35	312
34	381
33	448
32	513
31	576
30	637
29	696
28	753
27	808

We find that $1537 = (39)^2 + (4)^2 = (31)^2 + (24)^2$. Now we wish to determine factors of 1537 from this information.

The basic procedure for $N = a^2 + b^2 = c^2 + d^2 =$ (possibly other sums of pairs of squares) is to first find the following values **f** and **g** [10,23,24]:

$$f = a - c$$

$$g = d - b$$

given here by $f = 8$ and $g = 20$. Now we find the quantity $(2cf + f^2) = (2bg + g^2) = 560$, and we divide this by $fg = 160$, giving $h = 3.5$ in this case. Then

$$N = (f^2 + g^2) \bullet (1 + h^2)/4$$

$$= (464 \bullet 13.25)/4$$

$$= 29 \bullet 53$$

We could have directly used the relation,

$$N = \frac{[(a - c)^2 + (b - d)^2] \bullet [(a + c)^2 + (b - d)^2]}{4(b - d)^2}$$

divvying up the denominator into products that divide the terms in the numerator.

Of course, we can use modular arithmetic sieves to decrease the number of possible values of **x**. Construction of a table such as Table 3 for the quantity $(N - x^2)$ would show that for $N = 1537 = 7 \bmod 9$, then $x = 0, 3, 4, 5,$ or $6 \bmod 9$, small relief in this case. However, for an $N = (5k' + 2)$, as here, **x** and **y** equal 1 or 4 mod 5, or in other words are of the form $(5p \pm 1)$. The fact that **N** is of the form $(4k + 1)$ does us no good, since all **x** mod 4 are possible, and since $N = (4k + 3)$ eliminates all **x** mod 4 we begin to see why we are limited to the former type.

We can also utilize two-digit endings of squares to determine possible sums of two squares that will give the last two digits of **N**. An analogous situation will be presented later, where this sieve is used in finding possible differences of two squares in Fermat's method.

As a comparison for this example, Fermat's method without the use of sieves takes only two steps before the factors 29 and 53 are found, although for widely differing factors or for prime numbers the methods are not as dissimilar.

For those of us still bothered by our inability to factor $N = 1457$ earlier with this method, despite showing it to be composite, we can turn to a more general form of Euler's factorization [7]. Here we find two representations of a number N in the form $(a^2 + Db^2)$ and $(c^2 + Dd^2)$. Since all numbers cannot be expressed in this form, we might veer off into this method when we find an entry $(N - x^2)$ which is a multiple of a square greater than 1. In our earlier sequence for $N = 1457$, we find in the second step that $N - (37)^2 = 88$, so that $N = (37)^2 + 22(2)^2$. Then we start a new series of tests to find a square result of $(N - 22x^2)$, beginning with x as the nearest integer less than or equal to $(N/22)^{1/2}$. Since we are decreasing in each step the initial value of $x = 8$, we have at most eight steps. In each step we can add $22(2x + 1)$ to our previous value of $(N - 22x^2)$. We begin with

$$\frac{x}{8} \quad \frac{N - 22x^2}{49}$$

and we stop immediately, having that $1457 = (37)^2 + 22(2)^2 = (7)^2 + 22(8)^2$.

To find the factors, we use the more general form of our previous technique—we find $\gcd(N, ad - bc)$ or $\gcd(N, ad + bc)$, each representing a factor. Here $(ad - bc) = 282$ and $(ad + bc) = 310$, which offers, after a quick solution using Euclid's Algorithm and its variations, the factors 47 and 31. (Try Fermat's method on this number!)

As a second general method, we can find pairs of squares that add to N of the form $(4k + 1)$ by finding pairs of triangular numbers that add to $N' = (N - 1)/4$ [10]. This derives from the algebraic equality,

$$(a + b + 1)^2 + (a - b)^2 = 4 \left\{ \frac{a(a + 1)}{2} + \frac{b(b + 1)}{2} \right\} + 1$$

Considering our earlier example of $N = 1537$, we have $N' = 384$. Then we find $(N' - t_x)$ for x up to $N'^{1/2}$.

x	$N' - t_x$
0	384
1	383 = 384 − 1
2	381 = 383 − 2
3	378 = 381 − 3
4	374
5	369
6	363
7	356
8	348
9	339
10	329
11	318
12	306
13	293
14	279
15	264
16	248
17	231
18	213
19	194

From endings and/or modular arithmetic sieves, we find that $378 = t_{27}$ and $231 = t_{21}$, again giving us the intermediate result $1537 = (39)^2 + (4)^2 = (31)^2 + (24)^2$.

There is an intriguing if not foolproof test for determining whether a given number N is prime if N is of the form $(4k + 1)$ and ends in 3 or 7 (e.g., 1433) [9,10]. Sadly enough, even when the trivial case of N ending in 5 is eliminated, this test applies to only one in four odd numbers.

First, we subtract the nearest square ending in 5 from $2N$, leaving a remainder r_0. These squares actually must end, as we know, in 25 and are the squares of numbers ending in 5, or in other words $(5a)^2$ with a odd, so our shortcut for squaring such numbers helps a great deal here. Then we find the following quantities:

$$r_1 = r_0 + 100(a - 1)$$

$$r_2 = r_1 + 100(a - 3)$$

$$r_3 = r_2 + 100(a - 5)$$

etc.

Now if one and only one square appears among these values, N is divisible by this square or is prime. Otherwise, N is composite.

For $N = 1433$, we have $2N = 2866$. The nearest square ending in 25 is found by determining a value b such that $b(b + 1)$ is nearest without exceeding 28. Therefore, $b = 4$ and $(45)^2 = 2025$. Continuing,

$$a = 9$$

$$r_0 = 2866 - 2025 = 841 = (29)^2$$

$$r_1 = 841 + 800 = 1641$$

$$r_2 = 1641 + 600 = 2241$$

$$r_3 = 2241 + 400 = 2641$$

$$r_4 = 2641 + 200 = 2841$$

There is only one square here, and 841 does not divide 1433, so 1433 is very probably prime according to this method. In fact, 1433 is prime, as we have seen.

For three-digit numbers this is very fast:

$$N = 713$$

$$2N = 1426$$

$$(35)^2 = 1225$$

$$r_0 = 201$$

$$r_1 = 801$$

No value of **r** is a square, so 713 is composite (713 = 23 • 31).

Composite integers are identified without fail in this test, but some numbers indicated as prime are actually composite. Taylor [9] notes that these latter anomalies ". . . are in general those integers which are multiples of primes of one of the forms (20**k** + 13) and (20**k** + 17) and also of one or more of the squares of 3, 7, 9, 11, 23, 27, . . . (i.e., (20**m** + 3,7,9,11)^2)." They include 153, 333, 477, 657, 833, and higher numbers. If the factors 3, 7, 11, and 13 are eliminated first, however, an anomaly will not surface until **N** equals 8993.

In closing, I mention for those interested in pursuing this subject on a computer or programmable calculator that summaries of factorization methods specifically designed for these instruments can be found in Riesel [7] and Blair [27]. Other methods suitable for hand calculations (or the above instruments) are given by Taylor [9] and Dickson [10].

A Factoring Game

Now I would like to take an extreme case of factorization to illustrate additional tests. While this will turn out to be unrealistic to perform on the spur of the moment, we can consider this factoring of a very large number to be a kind of game, and it's actually not a bad one at that if you're interested.

We would like to factor a given large number like 125,869. Since **N** is not divisible by 2, 3, 5, 7, 9, or 11, we begin using Fermat's method (my choice) with **x** = 355. Chapter 3 provides convenient methods for simple square root extraction. Here we would take (1258)$^{1/2}$ as roughly 35; then [1258 − (35)^2]/(2 • 35) as roughly 0.5. Appending 5 to 35 and checking the decimal point location, we arrive at 355 as **N**$^{1/2}$ to the nearest integer.

Unfortunately, we now find that the upper limit on **x** is (125869/25 + 6) = 5041, leaving an absolutely huge range to consider!

Undaunted, we find **N** mod 9 by casting out nines and arrive at 4, implying from Table 3 that we need consider only values of **x** ≡ 2 or 7 mod 9. We therefore decrease the number of possible values of **x** to roughly 521. We can then find **N** mod 5 = 4, giving **x** ≡ 0, 2, or 3 mod 5, and reducing the choices of **x** to around 313.

Finally, **N** mod 7 = 2, giving **x** ≡ 2, 3, 4, or 5 mod 7 and a net of about 179 choices.

Actually, since the formula for the upper limit on **x** is roughly inversely proportional to the lowest prime **p** not tested by standard divisibility tests,

$$x_{max} = \frac{N}{2p} + \frac{p}{2}$$

we can see that we really suffer in considering all primes in Fermat's method down to **p** = 13. Let us set **p** equal to 101 and perform two-digit divisibility tests for all primes below this if required. Then x_{max} = 679 and our original set reduces from 4686 to 324 values of **x**. Then applying our tests **N** mod 9, 8, 5, and 7 reduces the number of possible values of **x** to about 12.

We find no primes below 100 to divide **N**. However, to sequence through values of **x** to find the approximately 12 possible values from 355 to 679 that pass the sieves, and for each one square **x**, subtract **N** and check for endings of those that may be squares, explicitly finding square roots of those, is tedious still. Can we use more detective work to help us out?

Yes, we can. Let's see if we can find other sieves in a different manner. We know that **N** ends in 69 and that squares end in 00, **e**1, **e**4, 25, **d**6, or **e**9, where **e** is even and **d** is odd. What possible difference of squares end in 69? A quick check of Table 5 produces the number of possibilities for differences of squares ending in a particular digit.

Obviously, we could have been luckier here. The four possibilities for a difference ending in 9 can be easily deduced to be (00 – **e**1), (**e**4 – **e**5), (25 – **d**6) and (**e**9 – 00).

For numbers ending in 69, we can reduce the choices to (25 – 56) and (69 – 00). We can now find what **x** must end in to arrive at these endings. It turns out that for each of the 22 possibilities of two-digit endings for a square x^2, there are four possible two-digit endings of **x**, except for 00 and 25, which have ten (numbers ending in 0 and 5, respectively). For the former, when one two-digit ending, say x_1, is found, the other three can be found as $|100 - x_1|$, $|50 - x_1|$ and $|50 + x_1|$, where here the vertical bars indicate the absolute value of the term inside. This follows from the equations,

Table 5
Differences of Squares Ending in Particular Digits

b\a	0	1	4	5	6	9	Digit	Number of Possibilities
0	0	1	4	5	6	9	9	4
1	9	0	3	4	5	8	8	2
4	6	7	0	1	2	5	7	2
5	5	6	9	0	1	4	6	4
6	4	5	8	9	0	3	5	6
9	1	2	5	6	7	0	4	4
			a − b				3	2
							2	2
							1	4
							0	6

$$(100 - x_1)^2 = 10000 - 200x_1 + x_1^2$$

$$(50 \pm x_1)^2 = 2500 \pm 100x_1 + x_1^2$$

For example, we know that $(13)^2 = 169$, which ends in 69. Therefore, other two-digit endings that when squared produce an ending of 69 are $(100 - 13)$, $(50 + 13)$, and $(50 - 13)$.

We can, then, find possible endings of **x** for each ending of x^2. We are in reality performing a manual mod 100 sieve.

x^2-ending	x-ending
69	13,37,63,87
25	05,15,25,35,45,55,65,75,85,95

Notice that we can already see that the sieves **x** mod 8 = 1, 3, 5, or 7 and **x** mod 5 = 0, 2, or 3 are useless here, since they can be determined by these endings. More work is still necessary. While it may seem lucky to have isolated the endings to particular numbers instead of e4, for example, the value 25 with its ten entries above hurts us considerably.

In reality we don't need to construct the above x-endings as a table in our mind, but rather find each x-ending one at a time and operate the rest of our procedure on them individually. We then end up sequencing one line at a time through Table 6. Notice that $355 \leq x \leq 679$.

Now by using endings we not only have reduced the number of possible values of x to four, but we have also identified them without testing intermediate values. At this point, if we want to avoid squaring the remaining x-values, it is appropriate to check y^2 for any reduction of the y-values as well.

Fortunately, this is very easy. Since adding **N** mod **m** is the same thing as subtracting $(\mathbf{m} - \mathbf{N})$ mod **m**, then we can use Table 3 for x mod **m** and use the values derived for the complement of **N** mod **m**, thereby giving us general results for a number $(\mathbf{y}^2 + \mathbf{N})$ mod **m**. Therefore, without actually doing any divisibility tests we immediately know that

y mod 9 = 0,3,6   from entry for N mod m = 9 – 4 = 5

y mod 8 = 2,6   from entry for N mod m = 8 – 5 = 3

y mod 5 = 0,1,4   from entry for N mod m = 5 – 4 = 1

y mod 7 = 0,3,4   form entry for N mod m = 7 – 2 = 5

Of these, we are interested in y mod 5 and y mod 8, since divisibility by 5 and 4 is obtainable from the two-digit ending.

Looking at endings for y^2, we can deduce that a y^2-ending of 56 arises from y-endings of 16, 34, 66, and 84. Of these, the above two sieves limit y-endings to 34 and 66.

We can now take each of the four values of x remaining after our sieve and find possible values of y. Remember that $(x - y) > 100$. In addition, we know that $(x^2 - N) = y^2$, and this must hold up to all divisibility tests.

For x = 605, we know that $(x^2 - N)$ mod 9 = $[(2)^2 - 4]$ mod 9 = 0; because of the earlier x mod 9 sieve, all of these values of x will give this result. Therefore, only y = 234 is possible, since the nines test on the ending 34 implies an initial digit of 2 for the

Table 6
Modular Sieve Results for *N* = 125869

$x^2 - y^2$ Ending	x^2 Ending	x Ending	Sieve x mod 9 = 2,7	Additional Sieve x mod 7 = 2,3,4,5
69–00	69	13	—	
		37	637	—
		63	—	
		87	587	—
25–56	25	05	605	605
		15	515	515
		25	425	425
		35	—	
		45	—	
		55	—	
		65	565	565
		75	475	—
		85	385	—
		95	—	

range $0 < y < 505$. An ending of 66 produces no initial digit in this range. As $y = 234$ seems a likely possibility, we cast out elevens to check it again, producing $(x^2 - N)$ mod $11 = [(0)^2 - 7]$ mod $11 = 5$. The y-value 234 is now eliminated because $(234)^2$ mod $11 = 9$; thus x cannot be 605.

For $x = 515$, again only $y = 234$ is possible and is eliminated by the elevens test.

For $x = 425$, we find $y = 234$ does indeed pass the elevens test.

For $x = 565$, we find that $y = 234$ passes the elevens test as well.

We can perform other divisibility tests if we still want to avoid squaring three-digit numbers. As mentioned earlier, a good one is for 37.

$$(x^2 - N) \bmod 37 = [(425)^2 - 125869] \bmod 37$$

$$= [(-19)^2 - (014,-019)] \bmod 37$$

$$= [367 - (-19 + 14)] \bmod 37$$

$$= 366 \bmod 37 = 33$$

As a reminder, we dropped multiples of 111 out of each triplet and added each triplet to the triplet to the right of it. Now $(234)^2$ mod 37 = $(12)^2$ mod 37 = 33 as well.

If we repeat this for x = 565, we find $(x^2 - N)$ mod 37 = 31 and the failure of y to pass this sieve eliminates this possibility.

We've danced around the result for quite a while now and we know that x = 425, y = 234 is strongly indicated, since out of two cases like this the odds of one passing the divisibility test for 37 without being a solution is one in 18.5. We could square this out if we wanted, but let's continue to be stubborn about this and assert with great confidence that $(425 - 234)$ = 191 and $(425 + 234)$ = 659 are factors of 125869, which indeed they are.

Without using modular arithmetic sieves, how many steps would we have had to perform using Fermat's method to find these factors? We earlier had the expression $(1 - k)^2 \, N^{1/2}/(2k)$ for the number of steps, given that the lower factor a = $kN^{1/2}$. Here a = 191 and we find k = 0.538, giving 70 steps (after the initial value of y is obtained). Using triangular numbers, which shine when factors are disparate, we require 18 steps without sieves.

Bibliography

1. Robert E. Moritz, *Memorabilia Mathematica*, Macmillan, New York, 1914, p. 6.
2. Karl Menninger, *Calculator's Cunning*, Basic Books, New York, 1964, pp. 42–44, 55–64, 77–82, 97–110.
3. Steven B. Smith, *The Great Mental Calculators*, Columbia University Press, New York, 1983, pp. 111–114, 145.
4. H. E. Licks, *Recreations in Mathematics*, D. Van Nostrand, New York, 1921, pp. 7–9.
5. D. E. Smith, *History of Mathematics Vol. II: Special Topics of Elementary Mathematics*, Dover, New York, 1925, pp. 122–123.
6. Donald E. Knuth, *The Art of Computer Programming Vol. II: Seminumerical Algorithms*, Addison-Wesley, Reading, 1969, pp. 244, 258–259, 293–300, 342–347.
7. Hans Riesel, *Prime Numbers and Computer Methods for Factorization*, Birkhäuser, Boston, 1985, pp. 151–166, 184–190, 223–245, 318–323, 349–352.
8. P. H. Nygaard, "Repeating Decimals," *The Mathematics Teacher*, 31 (1938) pp. 316–321.

9. L. F. Taylor, *Numbers,* Faber and Faber, London, 1970, pp. 16–42, 79, 107–131.

10. Leonard E. Dickson, *History of the Theory of Numbers Vol. I, II,* Publication No. 256, Carnegie Institute of Washington, Washington, 1919, pp. 159–179, 225–257, 357–374, 426.

11. A. C. Aitken, "The Art of Mental Calculation; with Demonstrations," *Transactions of the Society of Engineers,* 44 (1954) pp. 295–309.

12. Derrick Henry Lehmer, "A Cross-Division Process and Its Application to the Extraction of Roots," *American Mathematical Monthly,* 33 (1926) pp. 198–206.

13. M. Abromowitz and I. A. Stegun, *Handbook of Mathematical Functions,* Applied Mathematics Series, Vol. 55, National Bureau of Standards, Washington, 1964, reprinted by Dover Publications, New York, 1972, p. 21.

14. J. V. Uspensky, *Theory of Equations,* McGraw-Hill, New York, 1948, pp. 159–164.

15. Ladis D. Kovach, "Ancient Algorithms Adapted to Modern Computers," *Mathematics Magazine,* 37 (1964) pp. 159–165.

16. A. W. Goodman and W. M. Zaring, "Euclid's Algorithm and the Least-Remainder Algorithm," *American Mathematical Monthly,* 59 (1952) pp. 156–159.

17. V. C. Harris, "An Algorithm for Finding the Greatest Common Divisor," *The Fibonacci Quarterly,* 8 (1970) pp. 102–103.

18. Charles F. Winans, "Short Cuts for Testing Divisibility," *Journal of Recreational Mathematics,* 8 (1975–6) pp. 252–254.

19. W. J. Langford, "Tests for Divisibility," *The Mathematical Gazette,* 48 (1974) pp. 186–188.

20. M. J. DeLeon, "A Simple Proof of an Old Divisibility Test," *Journal of Recreational Mathematics,* 11 (1978–9) pp. 186–189.

21. David M. Burton, "Devising Divisibility Tests," *Journal of Recreational Mathematics,* 9 (1976–7) pp. 258–260.

22. Charles Vanden Eynden, "Flipping a Coin over the Telephone," *Mathematics Magazine,* 62 (1989) pp. 167–172.

23. George P. Loweke, *The Lore of Prime Numbers,* Vantage, New York, 1982, pp. 60–64.

24. Kenneth H. Rosen, *Elementary Number Theory and Its Applications,* Addison-Wesley, Reading, 1984, pp. 79–85.

25. H. Davenport, *The Higher Arithmetic,* Hutchinson, London, 1962, pp. 32–35.

26. R. P. Burn, A *Pathway Into Number Theory*, Cambridge University Press, Cambridge, 1982, pp. 115–119.
27. W. D. Blair, et al., "Factoring Large Numbers on a Pocket Calculator," *American Mathematical Monthly*, 93 (1986) pp. 802–808.

Roots

The real test of ability to do square, cube or any other root is, in my view, to have a number proposed that is not an exact power, and to be asked to give the answer to several decimals; but this type of question you will hardly find in the published records.

A. C. Aitken (1954) [1]

Although extracting integer roots of powers is a common practice of lightning calculators, deriving roots of numbers that are not perfect powers is historically much more rare. This chapter is concerned with the much more practical problem of determining roots of such diverse numbers. Nonetheless, we will first touch on methods for perfect powers, if only to satisfy curiosity on the subject.

Roots of Perfect Powers

Roots of perfect powers, particularly odd powers, offer distinct advantages to the calculator. Briefly, it is well known that for a power of order $(4k + 1)$, with k a positive integer, the root will contain the same units digit as the power. For a power of order $(4k + 3)$, the root will contain a unique units digit for each unit digit of the power. For a three-digit root of any odd perfect power, the leading digit can be inferred from memorized or estimated ranges of such powers. With the knowledge of the units digit, the middle digit can be derived by casting out nines and/or elevens.

To illustrate, suppose we are given 6657793506607 as the fifth power of a number and our task is to find the fifth root. Now, the given number is about 670×10^{10} and we find (or memorize) ranges for the first digit of the fifth root. We see that $(300)^5 = 243 \times 10^{10}$ and $(400)^5 = 1024 \times 10^{10}$, so the answer is a three digit number with 3 as its first digit. Since the order of the root, 5, is of the form $(4k + 1)$, we immediately know that the last digit is the same as that for the given number, or 7. To determine the middle digit **a**, we use the nines test and, if needed, the elevens test:

$$6657793506607 \bmod 9 = (\ 6 + 6 + 5 + 7 + 7 + 9 + 3 + 5$$

$$+ 0 + 6 + 6 + 0 + 7)\ \bmod 9$$

$$= 4$$

We know, then, that $(3\mathbf{a}7)^5 \bmod 9 = 4$.
Now we want a number less than nine that, when raised to the fifth power, will leave a remainder of 4 in the nines test.

Number n	Nines test result on n^5
0	0
1	1
2	5
3	0
4	7
5	2
6	0
7	4
8	8

We could have memorized this table or generated it on the spot. To do this, we remember that we can always reduce intermediate values in our calculation by the nines test. For example, for **n** = 5,

$n^2 \bmod 9 = (5)^2 \bmod 9 = 7$

$n^4 \bmod 9 = (7)^2 \bmod 9 = 4$

$n^5 \bmod 9 = (5 \bullet 4) \bmod 9 = 2$

The only ambiguity in this test is for a result of zero, which corresponds to $n = 0$, 3, and 6. The elevens test can then be used to distinguish between these cases. For cube roots, the elevens test is preferable up front, because it provides unique results for every $n < 11$.

In our case, we have now deduced that $3a7 \bmod 9 = 7$, or $(3 + a + 7) \bmod 9 = 7$. Simple inspection shows that $a = 6$, so we arrive at 367 as the fifth root of 66577993506607.

For roots containing more (say, **m**) digits, the logarithm may be calculated of the first $(m - 2)$ digits of the power. The result is then divided by the order of the power, as we do when using logarithms, and then converted back into the initial digits of the root. The last two digits are then derived from the uniqueness of the units digit and casting out nines or elevens, as before.

For the practiced calculator, the task can be simplified by memorizing tables of two-digit or three-digit endings of powers. For most roots, the endings are not unique, though, and require a subsequent process of elimination. Nonetheless, the huge ranges of powers that can be considered can make the extraction of perfect roots seem amazing. For example, extracting a three-digit cube root, which as described above is trivial, can be performed on numbers up to $(999)^3 = 997002999$. All three-digit roots of odd powers are equally trivial, and the ranges of numbers become incredible for high powers. Smith [2] provides an excellent review of these techniques and the use of endings to ease multidigit integer roots.

Particular Square Root Methods

Since we rarely find ourselves extracting roots of powers known to be perfect, a more desirable algorithm would extract noninteger roots as well. A few of the better methods of obtaining a noninteger root (and to be precise, an integer root as well) were described by Alexander Craig Aitken, considered by Smith to be "one of the greatest mental calculators who ever lived [2]."

In a passage from Aitken's address to the Society of Engineers [1], part of which can be found in Smith [2] as well, we find a presentation of six ways an experienced calculator might approximate the square root of 51 (or 7.141428428543 . . .):

1. Take an initial estimate of the square root of 51, or $(51)^{1/2}$, as 7. The average of 7 (or 49/7) and 51/7 provides a much better estimate, 50/7 = 7.1429. . . .
2. Take 50/7 as the new initial estimate. The average of this and 51/(50/7) is 7.141429. . . .
3. Take the repeating decimal 7.141414 . . . as a new initial estimate. Referring to our discussion in Chapter 2, we know this to be the fraction 707/99. The average of this and 51/(707/99) is 7.14142842857 . . . , accurate to eleven digits.
4. Return to our estimate of 50/7, which was the average of our initial estimate of 7 (or 49/7) and 51/7. Their ratio is 49/51 and each "deviates" by one part in 50. Reduce 50/7 by one part in $2(50)^2$, or one part in 5000, arriving at 4999/700 = 7.1414285. . . .
5. Divide the interval from 49 to 51 into fourths and multiply 7 by the third quarter divided by the first, giving $7(50\frac{1}{2}/49\frac{1}{2})$ = 7.141414141414. . . . Alternatively, find $(51/7) \bullet (49\frac{1}{2}/50\frac{1}{2})$ = 7.141442715700. . . . Their average is even better, being, in fact, that found in method 3.
6. Using "subtler and more powerful approximations still," reduce 50/7 as in method 4 by one part in $4999\frac{1}{2}$ rather than one part in 5000, giving 7.141428428557 . . . , "so committing an error of 1 in 500,000,000,000. This is an extreme approximation for [a] square root; and I have never gone beyond it in mental calculation."

While Aitken does not elaborate in his presentation on the bases for his methods, we can with some effort reconstruct the reasoning behind them. To begin, we make use of a concept formulated by Heron of Alexandria (c. 50?) and most likely by the Babylonians of 1700 B.C. [3,4]. Aitken (and Smith) did explicitly refer to this method.

We reason here that if a number **N** is deduced to have an approximate root **a** (say, one that is too low), then the quantity **N/a** provides a number that will lie on the other (high) side of the root $N^{1/2}$. Therefore, a better approximation to $N^{1/2}$ will be the average of **a** and **N/a**. This procedure can be iterated and is of second order, i.e., the number of correct digits approximately doubles with each iteration [5–7]. We then have the iterative relation with **n** = 0,1,2, . . .

$$a_{n+1} = \frac{a_n + (N/a_n)}{2} \tag{4}$$

$$= a_n + a_n \frac{N - a_n^2}{2a_n^2}$$

This is actually a special case of the well-known Newton-Raphson method of finding simple, real roots of a real equation of the form f(**a**) = 0 [3,8–11]:

$$a_{n+1} = a_n - \frac{f(a_n)}{f'(a_n)} \tag{5}$$

where $f'(a_n)$ denotes the first derivative of f(**a**) with respect to **a** evaluated at a_n. For f(**a**) = a^p – **N** = 0,

$$a_{n+1} = a_n + a_n \frac{N - a_n^p}{pa_n^p} \tag{6}$$

which reduces to Equation 4 when the order of the root **p** = 2. Aitken derived his first three estimates from his initial approximations using one iteration of the Newton-Raphson method.

There are several ways of deriving the Newton-Raphson relation (Equation 5). A nongraphical derivation follows from the expansion of a function f(**a**) into a Taylor series:

$$f(a) = f(a_n) + f'(a_n) \bullet (a - a_n) + \frac{f''(a_n)}{2!} \bullet (a - a_n)^2 + \ldots$$

We can truncate this after the second derivative term and set $f(a) = 0$. Casting the formula in an iterative form to approach $f(a)$, we then have

$$f(a_n) + f'(a_n) \bullet (a_{n+1} - a_n) + \frac{f''(a_n)}{2} \bullet (a_{n+1} - a_n)^2 = 0$$

which can be rewritten as

$$a_{n+1} - a_n = \frac{-f(a_n)}{f'(a_n) + (a_{n+1} - a_n)^2 \, f''(a_n)/2} \tag{7}$$

This reduces to Equation 5 when the second derivative term in the denominator is neglected.

Certainly more satisfying (if less general) is a simpler derivation for roots of order p. Here, for an error e_n, a root $a = a_n + e_n$, and an order $p = 2$ (i.e., a square root),

$$a^2 - N = 0$$

$$(a_n + e_n)^2 - N = 0$$

$$a_n^2 + 2a_n e_n + e_n^2 - N = 0$$

$$e_n = \frac{N - a_n^2}{2a_n + e_n}$$

or, ignoring the e_n term in the denominator and setting $a_{n+1} = a_n + e_n$,

$$a_{n+1} = a_n + \frac{N - a_n^2}{2a_n}$$

which is identical to Equation 6 for $p = 2$.

To continue to Aitken's fourth method, we can perform a second iteration of Equation 4. Since $a_0 = 7$ led to a value a_1 best represented as a fraction $50/7$, it is useful to rewrite Equation 4 for $a_n = s/t$:

$$a_{n+1} = a_n + a_n \bullet \frac{t^2 N - s^2}{2s^2}$$

Then,

$$a_2 = \frac{50}{7} + \frac{50}{7} \bullet \frac{49 \bullet 51 - 2500}{2 \bullet 2500}$$

$$= 50/7 + (50/7) \bullet (-1/5000)$$

$$= 7.1414285\ldots$$

which is Aitken's fourth estimate.

We can also develop an improved version of the Newton-Raphson method. This variation has been discovered many times and bears several names; we will adopt the more common and appropriate designation of Halley's method, referring to Edmond Halley (1656?–1743) of comet fame [3,9,12–15].

In Equation 7 we can replace the $(a_{n+1} - a_n)$ term in front of the second derivative $f''(a_n)$ in the denominator with the approximation found in Equation 5, which we obtained by ignoring this term completely. This is Halley's formula:

$$a_{n+1} = a_n - \frac{2f(a_n)\ f'(a_n)}{2f'(a_n)^2 - f(a_n)\ f''(a_n)}$$

For $f(a) = a^p - N = 0$, we arrive at a third-order formula for finding the pth root of N [6,16,17]:

$$a_{n+1} = a_n \bullet \frac{(p - 1)a_n^p + (p + 1)N}{(p + 1)a_n^p + (p - 1)N}$$

or,

$$a_{n+1} = a_n \bullet \frac{a_n^p + \dfrac{p+1}{2p} \bullet (N - a_n^p)}{a_n^p + \left(1 - \dfrac{p+1}{2p}\right) \bullet (N - a_n^p)} \tag{8}$$

For the square root, we have **p** = 2 and

$$a_{n+1} = a_n \bullet \frac{a_n^2 + (3/4) \bullet (N - a_n^2)}{a_n^2 + (1/4) \bullet (N - a_n^2)}$$

Returning to our example **N** = 51 and a_0 = 7, we obtain the first approximation in Aitken's fifth estimate:

$$a_1 = 7\,(50\tfrac{1}{2}/49\tfrac{1}{2}) = 7.14141414\dots$$

We can now rewrite Equation 8 for $a_n' = N/a_n^{p-1}$ as

$$a_{n+1}' = a_n' \bullet \frac{\dfrac{N^p}{a_n^{p(p-1)}} + \dfrac{p+1}{2p} \bullet \left(N - \dfrac{N^p}{a_n^{p(p-1)}}\right)}{\dfrac{N^p}{a_n^{p(p-1)}} + \left(1 - \dfrac{p+1}{2p}\right) \bullet \left(N - \dfrac{N^p}{a_n^{p(p-1)}}\right)}$$

After some algebra we arrive at the relation

$$a_{n+1}' = a_n' \bullet \frac{N^{2-p}a_n^{p(p-1)} + (1 - (p+1)/2p) \bullet (N - N^{2-p}a_n^{p(p-1)})}{N^{2-p}a_n^{p(p-1)} + ((p+1)/2p) \bullet (N - N^{2-p}a_n^{p(p-1)})}$$

$$\tag{9}$$

For **p** = 2, the extensive term multiplying a_n' is the reciprocal of the corresponding term in Equation 8. This provides us with the second approximation by Aitken in the fifth estimate:

$$a_n' = (51/7) \bullet (49\tfrac{1}{2}/50\tfrac{1}{2}) = 7.14142715700\dots$$

Now Equation 4 gives a better approximation as the average of a_n and N/a_n. For $a_1 = 7(50\tfrac{1}{2}/49\tfrac{1}{2})$, then $N/a_1 = a_1'$ and we culminate in the fifth estimate,

$$a_2 = (a_1 + a_1^!)/2 = 7.14142842857\ldots$$

correct to eleven digits.

Returning to Equation 8, we can transform the third-order relation to one that eases our later calculations:

$$a_{n+1} = a_n + 2a_n \bullet \frac{N - a_n^p}{(p + 1)a_n^p + (p - 1)N}$$

We now recognize this as second-order Equation 6 if we set **N** equal to a_n^p in the denominator.

Use of this algorithm requires nontrivial division when **N** is a multidigit number or **p** is larger than 2. Given this, we can write the relation in a form suitable for a_n being a fraction **s/t**:

$$a_{n+1} = a_n + 2a_n \bullet \frac{t^pN - s^p}{(p + 1)s^p + (p - 1)t^pN}$$

or, for **p** = 2,

$$a_{n+1} = a_n + 2a_n \bullet \frac{t^2N - s^2}{3s^2 + t^2N}$$

Again, for a_1 = 50/7,

$$a_2 = 50/7 + 2(50/7) \bullet \frac{49 \bullet 51 - (50)^2}{3(50)^2 + 49 \bullet 50}$$

$$= 50/7 + (50/7) \bullet (-2/9999)$$

$$= 7.141428428557\ldots$$

which, since we are reducing 50/7 by one part in $4999\frac{1}{2}$, is apparently the extreme approximation used by Aitken in the sixth estimate to eleven digit accuracy.

The Chebyshev Correction

We can add at this point a further generalization of the Newton-Raphson method discovered by P. L. Chebyshev (1821–1894). His paper on this subject earned a silver medal in a competition in 1840, but actually was not published until 1951 [3,11]. His iterative algorithm is a third-order one, meaning the error falls off cubically with each iteration, or equivalently, that the number of correct digits is approximately tripled with each iteration. The relation is given by

$$a_{n+1} = a_n - \frac{f(a_n)}{f'(a_n)} - \left(\frac{f(a_n)}{f'(a_n)}\right)^2 \bullet \frac{f''(a_n)}{2f'(a_n)}$$

Notice that this amounts to subtracting a term in each iteration from the Newton-Raphson algorithm. For $f(a) = a^p - N = 0$,

$$\left(\frac{f(a_n)}{f'(a_n)}\right)^2 \bullet \frac{f''(a_n)}{2f'(a_n)} = \left(\frac{a_n^p - N}{pa_n^{p-1}}\right)^2 \bullet \frac{p(p-1)\ a_n^{p-2}}{2pa_n^{p-1}}$$

$$= \frac{p-1}{2p^2 a_n} \bullet \left(\frac{N - a_n^p}{a_n^{p-1}}\right)^2 \tag{10}$$

For $p = 2$, this correction term is given by

$$\frac{1}{8a_n} \bullet \left(\frac{N - a_n^2}{a_n}\right)^2$$

This method offers two advantages. It allows a preliminary estimate to be produced quickly using the Newton-Raphson method, and then improved afterwards with this correction if desired (merging the terms does not simplify the calculation). It also uses a divisor simpler than that used in Equation 8.

For an initial estimate of $a_0 = 7$ for $(51)^{1/2}$, we arrived at $a_1 = 50/7$ by using the Newton-Raphson technique. We can therefore improve this estimate by finding

$$a_1^| = 50/7 - \left(\frac{1}{8 \bullet 7}\right) \bullet \left(\frac{51 - (7)^2}{7}\right)^2$$

$$= 7.1413994$$

compared to $(51)^{1/2} = 7.14142843 \ldots$

which is an improvement over $50/7 = 7.142857 \ldots$ but poorer than two iterations of the Newton-Raphson method, which earlier yielded $7.1414285 \ldots$. As we will see for higher-order roots, however, two iterations of the Newton-Raphson method can in fact be prohibitive. For example, if a single-digit a_0 is used in the Newton-Raphson method to find a two-digit a_1 for the next iteration, then p doesn't have to be very large to prevent the next iteration a_2 from being calculated, particularly since a_1^p appears as a divisor. However, Chebyshev's additional term uses the original single-digit a_0 in its calculation.

A General Square Root Algorithm

The selection of $N = 51$ is a convenient, though illustrative, one for Aitken and in general the approximations become unmanageable very quickly. Incredibly, though, we can develop a method for mentally extracting square roots of more general multidigit numbers to greater and, with patience, even arbitrary precision.

To begin, we rearrange the second-order Equation 6 for $p = 2$ to express the amount b_n to be added to a_n in each iteration:

$$b_n = \frac{N - a_n^2}{2a_n}$$

Isaac Newton (1642–1727), incidentally, pointed out that hand calculations of square roots may be quickened if, after finding the square root the standard way to one-half the required number of digits, the remainder is divided by twice the existing calculated root to obtain the rest of the digits [4].

How good is this approximation? For our purposes, we can shift the decimal point (two places at a time) in the given number to scale the root to have two digits left of its decimal point. The decimal point can then be moved in the root (one place at a time) when we are finished. For example, if $N = 51$, we can let $N = 5100$ and find an approximate root 71.41, easily scaled back to 7.141. We do this because two-digit operations are most convenient in the general algorithm.

We can further assume for the time being that a two-digit approximation a_0 to $N^{1/2}$ is achievable by hook or by crook. Remember that we can square two-digit numbers fairly easily. One convenient technique for finding a_0 is to begin with a round number. For $N = 1867$,

$$1867 \approx 40 \bullet 46 = 1840$$

But $40 \bullet 46 = (43)^2 - (3)^2$, so

$$(1867)^{1/2} \approx 43 \text{ and } 1867 - (43)^2 = 27 - 9 = 18$$

Continuing now,

$$b_0 = \frac{18}{2 \bullet 43} = 9/43 = 0.20930 \ldots$$

and

$$a_0 + b_0 = 43.2093 \ldots \qquad \text{Actual: } 43.2088 \ldots$$

In general, the error in $(a_0 + b_0)$ is given by

$$\text{error} = (a_0 + b_0) - N^{1/2} = \frac{(N^{1/2} - a_0)^2}{2a_0}$$

Obviously, for large a_0 the error is small, as $-0.5 < (N^{1/2} - a_0) < 0.5$. As it turns out, for a two-digit integer a_0 we find that 98% of the time the quantity $(a_0 + b_0)$ will be accurate to two decimal places, and 50% of the time to three decimal places, offering four or five digit accuracy in a square root with a minimum of effort.

Since $(a_0 + b_0)$ will always be in excess, we can ask whether subtracting a number 0.000x before rounding, with x a digit, might improve the 50% average. In fact, it turns out that 0.0005 is the optimum amount to subtract. Therefore, by simply truncating the result to three decimal places rather than finding the fourth and rounding, the result will be accurate to three decimal places 61% of the time. The third decimal place will be within one of the correct digit 85% of the time.

The next iteration b_1, however, presents difficulties because $a_1 = a_0 + b_0$ is now a multidigit number; mentally calculating b_1 is generally prohibitive. We can in fact overcome this obstacle by developing an algorithm specifically for our purposes.

Let a_0 and b_n be two-digit numbers defined by

$$N^{1/2} = a_0 \mid b_0 \mid b_1 \mid b_2 \ldots \mid b_n \ldots$$

$$= a_0 + \sum_{k=0}^{\infty} 10^{-2k-2} b_k$$

where the decimal place lies between a_0 and b_0 and the symbol "$\mid b$" as before indicates that digits in b are melded into the term to the left to leave a two-digit value of b. Now,

$$10^{-2n-2} b_n = \frac{\left[N - \left(a_0 + \sum_{k=0}^{n-1} 10^{-2k-2} b_k \right)^2 \right]/2}{a_0 + \sum_{k=0}^{n-1} 10^{-2k-2} b_k}$$

If we limit b_n to two digits and approximate the denominator as a_0, we get

$$10^{-2n-2} b_n = \frac{\left[N - \left(a_0 + \sum_{k=0}^{n-1} 10^{-2k-2} b_k \right)^2 \right]/2}{a_0} - \frac{10^{-2n-2} r_n}{a_n}$$

where r_n is the remainder of the first term after dividing to two digits. Now,

$$10^{-2n-2}b_{n+1} = \frac{\left[N - \left(a_0 + \sum_{k=0}^{n} 10^{-2k-2}b_k \right)^2 \right]/2}{a_0} - \frac{10^{-2n-2}r_{n+1}}{a_0}$$

but,

$$N - \left(a_0 + \sum_{k=0}^{n} 10^{-2k-2}b_k \right)^2$$

$$= N - \left[\left(a_0 + \sum_{k=0}^{n-1} 10^{-2k-2}b_k \right) + 10^{-2n-2}b_n \right]^2$$

$$= N - \left(a_0 + \sum_{k=0}^{n-1} 10^{-2k-2}b_k \right)^2$$

$$- 2(10^{-2n-2}b_n) \bullet \left(a_0 + \sum_{k=0}^{n-1} 10^{-2k-2}b_k \right)$$

$$- 10^{-4n-4}b_n^2$$

$$= 2(10^{-2n-2})\, a_0 b_n + 2(10^{-2n-2})\, r_n$$

$$- 2(10^{-2n-2}b_n) \left(a_0 + \sum_{k=0}^{n-1} 10^{-2k-2}b_k \right)$$

$$- 10^{-4n-4}b_n^2$$

Therefore,

$$10^{-2n-4}b_{n+1} = \frac{10^{-2n-2}r_n - 10^{-2n-2}b_n \sum_{k=0}^{n-1} 10^{-2k-2}b_k - 10^{-4n-4}b_n^2/2}{a_0}$$

$$- \frac{10^{-2n-4}r_{n+1}}{a_0}$$

or,

$$b_{n+1} = \frac{100r_n - b_n \sum_{k=0}^{n-1} 10^{-2k}b_k - 10^{-2n}b_n^2/2}{a_0} - \frac{r_{n+1}}{a_0}$$

$$= 10^{2n+4} \frac{[N - (a_0 \mid b_0 \mid b_1 \ldots \mid b_n)^2]/2}{a_0}$$

This is perfectly general. The validity of the b_{n+1} value is not affected by the approximations of a_0 in the denominators of earlier b's. In fact, a_0 should be a rounded two-digit approximation to $N^{1/2}$ so b_0, which now may be positive or negative, has a magnitude of 50 or less.

Since we are concerned only with terms in the numerator that contribute to the division to two digits, we can shift other terms into the remainder term to be used in calculating b's of higher order. Conversely, since each b multiplies the remainder of the previous b by 100, we need to extract these shifted terms in the b at which they become significant (i.e., when the power of ten preceding the term is 0). Therefore, for n even,

$$b_{n+1} = \frac{100R_n - \sum_{k=0}^{n/2-1} b_{n-k}b_k - b_{n/2}^2/2}{a_0} + R_{n+1}$$

where R_n and R_{n+1} represent the new remainders of b_n and b_{n+1}, carrying with them the lower-order terms of previous b's that have not become significant yet in the division to two digits.

For n odd,

$$b_{n+1} = \frac{100R_n - \sum_{k=0}^{\frac{n}{2}-1} b_{n-k}b_k}{a_0} + R_{n+1}$$

Simply put, to find b_{n+1} we subtract from $100R_n$ pairwise multiplications of b starting from the outside ($b_0 b_n$) and working inward to the center; if one b is left in the center, we subtract $b^2/2$ as well. We then divide by a_0 to two digits and use the remainder for calculating the next b. Despite the heavy mathematical notation and derivation, the concept is quite simple, and is best understood by working through an actual calculation.

For example, to find the square root of 51, we first consider $(5100)^{1/2}$, which provides a two-digit a_0.

$$70 \bullet 72 = 4900 + 140 = 5040$$

giving $(71)^2 = 5040 + 1 = 5041$

Then,

$a_0 = 71$ with a remainder of 59

Root thus far: 71

$$b_0 = \frac{5900/2}{71} = 41 \qquad R_0 = 39$$

71 | 41

We now begin the algorithm.

$$b_1 = \frac{3900 - (41)^2/2}{71} = \frac{3059.5}{71} = 43 \qquad R_1 = 6.5$$

71 | 41 | 43

$$b_2 = \frac{650 - 41 \bullet 43}{71} = -\left(\frac{1113}{71}\right) = -(16 \text{ R } -23) = -16$$

$$R_2 = +23$$

71 | 41 | 43 | –16

$$b_3 = \frac{2300 - (-16) \bullet 41 - (43)^2/2}{71} = \frac{2031.5}{71} = 28$$

$$R_3 = 43.5$$

71 | 41 | 43 | –16 | 28

$$b_4 = \frac{4350 - 28 \bullet 41 - (-16) \bullet 43}{71} = \frac{3890}{71} = 54$$

$$R_4 = 56$$

71 | 41 | 43 | –16 | 28 | 54

$$b_5 = \frac{5600 - 54 \bullet 41 - 28 \bullet 43 - (-16)^2/2}{71} = \frac{2054}{71} = 28$$

$$R_5 = 66$$

71 | 41 | 43 | –16 | 28 | 54 | 28

In the last step, we could have taken $b_5 = 29$, $R_5 = -5$, but with the preponderance of positive **b**'s it seems likely that the numerator of b_6 will now be reduced to a number whose absolute value is less than $7100/2 = 3550$ (giving $b_6 \leq 50$), which is what we desire for two significant digit accuracy. In fact, the same philosophy was used in the two previous steps. If the absolute value of the numerator had turned out to be greater than 3550, giving a **b** ≥ 50, we would have simply backed up and increased or decreased the previous **b**, adjusting the previous remainder accordingly. This is most likely to occur when a_0 is small or when calculating higher-order **b**'s involving several terms in the numerator.

After all this buildup, it happens that I am mistaken and the numerator is still larger than 3550, but we're close enough to call it good.

$$b_6 = \frac{6600 - 28 \bullet 41 - 54 \bullet 43 + 16 \bullet 28}{71} = \frac{3578}{71} = 50$$

$$R_6 = 28$$

71 | 41 | 43 | –16 | 28 | 54 | 28 | 50

We could continue, but we're already well beyond the eleven digits obtained by Aitken. Adjusting the decimal point back to where it belongs, we get

$$(51)^{1/2} = 7.141428428542850\ldots$$

$$\text{Actual} = 7.141428428542850\ldots$$

An alternative in finding a_0 may be more convenient than what we did earlier:

$$(70)^2 = 4900$$

$$\frac{(5100 - 4900)/2}{70} = 1 \qquad \text{Remainder} = 30$$

Therefore $a_0 = 71$ and

$$b_0 = \frac{[30 - (1)^2/2]\,|\,00}{71} = 41 \qquad R_0 = 39$$

and we are back where we were before.

At any rate, we have succeeded in obtaining a sixteen-digit result with a reasonable number of two-digit multiplications and divisions. In fact, all **b**'s in this algorithm have magnitudes less than 50 (except where we let it go in b_6). Incidentally, did you notice that in b_4, for example, the terms $(-28) \bullet 41 + 16 \bullet 43$ can be reduced to $(-12) \bullet 41 + 32$? This is useful in b_3 through b_6. Two terms with multipliers of 28 also appear in the expression for b_6.

Throughout this discussion I have been careful not to drop the divisor 2 into the denominator for a reason. If we alter the division by a_0, we alter the remainder. Therefore, if the division is reduced by a factor **m**, we have to multiply the remainder by **m**. Also, it is incorrect to meld the **b**'s before the calculation ends. For example, the terms $43|-16$ cannot be converted to $42|84$ when calculating b_n's, even though this is what is done in the final melding.

It is also apparent that finding the square root of a four-digit number is no more difficult than for a two-digit number, since we expand the latter to four digits anyway. In fact, as in cross division, additional digits beyond the first four are simply taken pairwise, halved, and added to the numerator of the associated step. To demonstrate this, we will find the square root of 16460.89. Since $(13)^2 = 169$, we proceed from here:

$$164 - (13)^2 = -5$$

$$b_0 = \frac{(-500)/2 + 60/2}{13} = -(17 \text{ R} -1) = -17 \qquad R_0 = 1$$

$$13|-17$$

$$b_1 = \frac{100 + 89/2 - (-17)^2/2}{13} = 0 \qquad R_1 = 0$$

We find in this particular example that $(128.3)^2 = 16460.89$ exactly. Since $b_1 = 0$ and $R_1 = 0$, we see that in no later step can the numerator be other than 0 as $b_0 = -17$ will always be multiplied by a value $b = 0$.

Therefore, we have a useful method that offers no significant increase in effort between finding the square root of a one-digit number and that of a multidigit number. The increase in complexity with the number of root digits taken is quite low compared to that for the traditional square root method taught (at one time) in school. I encourage you to try extracting a sixteen-digit square root of 51 using the traditional method with paper and pencil; you will be astonished at the work involved. The integer-like character of this algorithm may also be useful for extracting square roots of extreme precision on small, integer-based computers.

I emphasize at this point what may have slipped by without notice, namely that we are for all practical purposes outstripping the capabilities of pocket calculators and virtually all commercial computer programs. The main reason I ended our calculations at sixteen digits is the difficulty I had in obtaining a verification of the answer beyond it! This is a double-precision floating point value. It takes a specially designed computer program to exceed this, and these are not routinely available. In my view, we can excel over the available instruments in extracting square roots in two areas. First, we can generally find an answer to five digits in less time than a calculator can be retrieved and worked, much less a computer. Second, with time we can find an answer to extreme precision, beyond what a calculator or typical computer would have the capability of doing without special software. I think we can take some satisfaction in this.

One expensive software package, a symbolic mathematics program, allowed me to arbitrarily define the precision of floating point values, and with it I obtained the square root of 51 to additional digits. The first 25 digits or so actually form an intriguing sequence of no significance that I am aware of: 7.1414284285428499979993998 . . . .

To my chagrin, but not unexpectedly, I found that the essence of this general method is given in other variations by Uspensky [18] and Lehmer [19], and perhaps others [20]. Lehmer derives the algorithm as a variant of cross division, run on the ten-digit mechanical computers of the day (1926). As in his cross division method, his algorithm contains internal checks on results and is therefore somewhat more involved than one designed for mental calculations. In addition, negative **b**'s are not considered, creating additional constraints on significant digits and requiring frequent multiplications by numbers of magnitude larger than 50. Also, since the divisor 2 appears in the denominator in determining quotients and remainders, the denominator generally consists of one more digit than necessary. Uspensky traces the algorithm to Fourier Division using single digits and again does not consider negative **b**'s.

To implement this algorithm using single-digit values of **b**, though, is more tedious and, in the end, problematic due to poorer resolution, as "backing up" can affect twice as many **b**'s. Uspensky discusses a convenient correction term when multiple **b**'s are altered. Three-digit values lead to frequent reversals to significantly adjust previous quotients. Two-digit values provide a nice compromise conducive to mental calculation.

In conclusion, I mention that for extracting the square root of a fraction, it is usually better to obtain a denominator that is a perfect square:

$$(2/7)^{1/2} = (14/49)^{1/2} = (14)^{1/2}/7$$

Beyond its immediate use, the ability to readily extract square roots offers an enormous advantage in developing other algorithms, including factoring methods that require an integral square to be identified, approximations of roots of higher order, very precise trigonometric approximations, and so forth. It is a very handy tool to master.

The Reciprocal Square Root

The reciprocal square root, or $N^{-1/2}$, can be calculated as a special case of the Newton-Raphson method applied to the equation $N - 1/a^p = 0$ [6,21]. Using Equation 5, we arrive at

$$a_{n+1} = a_n + \frac{a_n}{p} \bullet (1 - Na_n^p)$$

which we can write for $p = 2$ as

$$a_{n+1} = a_n + .5a_n(1 - Na_n^2)$$

a relation surprisingly free of divisions.

For example, let us find the value $(51)^{-1/2} = 0.1400280084028\ldots$ (a number, incidentally, as fortuitous for us as 51 was for Aitken). We can take $a_0 = 0.14$. Then

$$a_1 - a_0 = .5(.14)[1 - 51(.0196)]$$

$$= .07(.0004)$$

$$= .000028$$

$$a_1 = .140028$$

Furthermore, multiplying the above result by N provides an approximate value for $N^{1/2}$, obtained without significant division:

$$51(.140028) = 14.0028/2 + .140028$$

$$= 7.141428$$

Applying Halley's method to the equation $N - 1/a^p = 0$ results in

$$a_{n+1} = a_n + \frac{2a_n(1 - Na_n^p)}{2p - (p + 1) \bullet (1 - Na_n^p)}$$

Again, for $p = 2$, $N = 51$, and $a_0 = 0.14$,

$$a_1 = .14 + 1.12(10^{-4})/3.9988$$

$$= .1400280084023 \ldots$$

This is a stunning result, but the division is complicated. Perhaps the best approach is to factor out a 4 in the denominator and approximate $1/(1 - .0003)$ as $(1 + .0003)$. Then $a_1 = .14 + 2.8(10^{-5}) \bullet (1 + .0003) = .1400280084$.

Another alternative, generally more advantageous when a_0 is less accurate to the true value $N^{-1/2}$, is to derive Chebyshev's correction term for $f(a) = N - 1/a^p = 0$:

$$\left(\frac{f(a_n)}{f'(a_n)}\right)^2 \bullet \frac{f''(a_n)}{2f'(a_n)} = \frac{(N - a^{-p})^2}{p^2 a^{-2(p+1)}} \bullet \frac{- p(p + 1) a^{-(p+2)}}{2pa^{-(p+1)}}$$

$$= - \frac{p + 1}{2p^2} a_n(1 - Na_n^p)^2$$

For $p = 2$, $N = 51$ and $a_n = .14$, we can subtract this term from our earlier result from the Newton-Raphson method:

$$a_1' = .140028 + \frac{3}{2 \bullet 4} \, (.14)(.0004)^2$$

$$= .1400280084$$

accurate again to the last digit.

Cube Roots

Although the concept used in our last most general square root algorithm does not apply to extracting higher-order roots, we may revert to Equation 6 as a workable second-order approximation. We can rewrite this as

$$a_{n+1} = \frac{(p - 1) \, a_n + N/a_n^{p-1}}{p}$$

In other words, a_{n+1} is the weighted average of a_n and N/a_n^{p-1}.

For this relation, the error e_1 in a_1 is less than $(p - 1) \, e_0/p$. In general, the error in the nth iteration, for e_1 the error in a_1, is less than [22–24]:

$$\frac{(p - 1) \, e_{n-1}^2}{2a_{n-1}} \qquad \text{for } n > 1$$

Thus, after a_1 is found, the error in each step diminishes as the square of the previous error, defined as a second-order relation and approximately doubling the number of correct decimal places in each iteration.

As an example, consider $(119)^{1/3} = 4.9186847\ldots$, which we initially approximate as $a_0 = 5$. Then

$$a_1 = \frac{2 \bullet 5 + 119/(5)^2}{3} = 4.92$$

Choosing $a_0 = 4.9$ provides an $a_1 = 4.91875\ldots$, correct to four digits, but the division is more difficult.

Returning to the first weighted average $a_1 = 4.92$, we can increase our accuracy by subtracting Chebyshev's term, given in Equation 10, for $p = 3$:

$$a_1' = a_1 - \frac{1}{9a_0} \bullet \left(\frac{N - a_0^p}{a_0}\right)^2$$

$$= 4.92 - \frac{1}{9 \bullet 5} \bullet \left(\frac{119 - (5)^3}{(5)^2}\right)^2$$

$$= 4.91872$$

This result is more accurate than the Newton-Raphson method with $a_0 = 4.9$, and was obtained with much simpler division.

An alternate approach for cube roots involves, to gratefully adopt Aitken's terminology, the process of "thirding," a method corresponding to the quartering performed earlier for the square root [1]. Equation 8 provides a general method for the pth root, and for $p = 3$ it becomes

$$a_{n+1} = a_n \bullet \frac{a_n^3 + (2/3) \bullet (N - a_n^3)}{a_n^3 + (1/3) \bullet (N - a_n^3)}$$

Again choosing $a_0 = 5$ for $(119)^{1/3}$, we find $(N - a_0^3) = -6$ and

$$a_1 = 5 \bullet \frac{121}{123} = 4.9186992\ldots$$

which is a more accurate result than before, although this particular example involves a three-digit divisor.

The complementary process of "sixthing" operated on $a_0' = 119/(5)^2$ is another technique. Equation 9, the basis for the corresponding square root approximation, proves intractable for $p > 2$, so we turn again to Equation 8 with $a_{n+1} = N/a_{n+1}^{p-1}$:

$$a'_{n+1} = \frac{N}{a_n^{p-1}} \bullet \left(\frac{a_n^p + ((p + 1)/2p) \bullet (N - a_n^p)}{a_n^p + (1 - (p + 1)/2p) \bullet (N - a_n^p)} \right)^{1-p}$$

If we define $y = \frac{1}{2}(N + a_n^p)$,

$$a'_{n+1} = \frac{N}{a_n^{p-1}} \bullet \left(\frac{y - (1/2p) \bullet (N - a_n^p)}{y + (1/2p) \bullet (N - a_n^p)} \right)^{p-1}$$

$$= \frac{N}{a_n^{p-1}} \bullet \left(y^{p-1} - \frac{p - 1}{2p} y^{p-2}(N - a_n^p) + \frac{(p - 1)(p - 2)}{8p^2} \right.$$

$$\times \, y^{p-3}(N - a_n^p)^2 + \ldots \Bigg) \div \left(y^{p-1} - \frac{p - 1}{2p} y^{p-2}(N - a_n^p) \right.$$

$$\left. + \frac{(p - 1)(p - 2)}{8p^2} y^{p-3}(N - a_n^p)^2 + \ldots \right)$$

by the Binomial Theorem (discovered by Newton).

Now since y is the average of N and a_n^p and $(N - a_n^p)$ is assumed small in comparison to y, the terms after and including $(p - 1) \times (p - 2) \, y^{p-3}(N - a_n^p)^2/8_p^2$ can be eliminated with minor error, leaving

$$a'_{n+1} = \frac{N}{a_n^{p-1}} \bullet \frac{y^{p-1} - \dfrac{p - 1}{2p} y^{p-2}(N - a_n^p)}{y^{p-1} + \dfrac{p - 1}{2p} y^{p-2}(N - a_n^p)}$$

which reduces to

$$a'_{n+1} = \frac{N}{a_n^{p-1}} \bullet \frac{a_n^p + \dfrac{1}{2p}(N - a_n^p)}{a_n^p + \left(1 - \dfrac{1}{2p}\right) \bullet (N - a_n^p)} \tag{11}$$

For **p** = 3, we have the sixthing process:

$$a'_{n+1} = \frac{N}{a_n^2} \bullet \frac{a_n^3 + (1/6) \bullet (N - a_n^3)}{a_n^3 + (5/6) \bullet (N - a_n^3)}$$

Why would anyone use sixthing when any $(N - a_n^3)$ divisible by 6 would also be divisible by 3? The answer is that sometimes the numerator and/or the denominator is simpler in sixthing, and also for very small error in a_{n+1}, the weighted average of the two techniques provides even greater accuracy.

Indeed, $N = 119$ was chosen to demonstrate the first advantage. For $a'_0 = 119/(5)^2$,

$$a'_1 = (119/25) \bullet (124/120) = 4.76 + 4.76(1/30)$$

$$= 4.9186667 \ldots$$

Aitken remarked in 1954 that he was not aware that sixthing had ever received notice before, although he gave no basis for it.

We can expect marginally better accuracy (perhaps to the fifth decimal place) if we find the weighted average of a_1 and a'_1:

$$\frac{2a_1 + a'_1}{3} = 4.9186 + 10^{-4}(1/3) \bullet [2(.99) + .67]$$

$$= 4.918688 \ldots$$

an approximation accurate to six digits.

Again, an alternate cube root formula [25] can be derived from

$$(a_n - N^{1/3})^3 = a_n^3 - N - 3a_n^2 N^{1/3} + 3a_n N^{2/3}$$

Now an approximation a_{n+1} satisfies

$$a_{n+1}^2 - a_n a_{n+1} + (a_n^3 - N)/3a_n = 0$$

giving, for $0 < a_n^3 < 4N$,

$$a_{n+1} = \frac{1}{2}\left[a_n + \left(\frac{4N - a_n^3}{3a_n}\right)^{1/2} \right]$$

The square root term to several places is manageable (using methods given earlier) and the formula is of third order.

For $N = 119$ and $a_0 = 5$,

$$a_1 = \tfrac{1}{2} \left[5 + \left(\frac{476 - 125}{3 \cdot 5} \right)^{1/2} \right]$$

$$= \tfrac{1}{2} \, [5 + (351/15)^{1/2}]$$

$$= \tfrac{1}{2} \, [5 + (23.4)^{1/2}]$$

$$= \tfrac{1}{2} \, (5 + 4.837355 \ldots)$$

$$= 4.918677 \ldots$$

again accurate to six digits (and better here than thirding or sixthing alone). In general, this method offers the advantage of a smaller divisor, $3a_n$, compared to roughly a_n^3 in thirding or sixthing (unless simplification is possible, as for $N = 119$). The obvious disadvantage lies in evaluating the square root. However, the insensitivity of the square root algorithm to the number of digits, as opposed to division by a multidigit number, may quickly propel this method into the forefront when a_n contains two or more digits.

If we really don't mind taking a square root (as by using the general square root algorithm given earlier) we can achieve even greater accuracy in a cube root without raising a_n's to powers and with division limited to that within the square root extraction process [26]. To do this, we perform the Newton-Raphson procedure not on the equation $a^3 - N = 0$, but on the equation $a^{3/2} - N^{1/2} = 0$ or $a^{3/4} - N^{1/4} = 0$. We then produce

$$a_{n+1} = (1/3) \cdot [2(N/a_n)^{1/2} + a_n] \tag{12}$$

and

$$a_{n+1} = (1/3) \cdot [4(Na_n)^{1/4} - a_n] \tag{13}$$

both more accurate than the original Newton-Raphson iteration.

For $N = 119$ and $a_0 = 5$, Equations 12 and 13 yield $a_1 = 4.91901624 \ldots$ and $a_1 = 4.91851830 \ldots$ respectively, compared to the actual value of 4.91868473 . . . . For a_0 = 4.9, we obtain a_1 = 4.91870254 . . . and a_1 = 4.91867584 . . . . However, notice that if we can manage to multiply N and a_n in Equation 13 for a highly accurate a_n or at least divide N by a_n in Equation 12, we are on the way to an extremely accurate (if time-consuming) cube root. This assumes that we are comfortable taking square roots to several places (and I would rather extract a square root than perform a long division).

For example, we can find 119(4.92) = 119 • (5 − .08) = 585.48, and from Equation 13,

$$a_1 = (1/3) \bullet [4(585.48)^{1/4} - 4.92]$$

$$= 4.91868469 \ldots$$

accurate to eight digits.

While not applicable to N = 119, we can sometimes recognize that by multiplying or dividing N by the cube of a small number, or the ratio of cubes of small numbers, we can arrive at a number close to a cube. For example, for N = 91, a number distant from the nearest cubes (64 and 125), we can multiply N by 8 to arrive at 728, very close indeed to 729, the cube of 9. Therefore, $N^{1/3}$ is approximately 9/2 = 4.5, where 2 is the cube root of 8. Better yet, we can take a weighted average:

$$728/(9)^2 = 8.98765 \ldots$$

$$2N^{1/3} \approx (2 \bullet 9 + 8.98765 \ldots)/3$$

$$N^{1/3} \approx 3 + 8.98765/6$$

$$= 4.4979424 \ldots \text{ compared to } 4.4979408 \ldots$$

Failing this, we can often divide a number by 2 or 5 to produce a new number close to a cube. We then find the approximate cube root of this new number, and adjust the result by multiplying by $(2)^{1/3}$ = 1.25992 . . . $\approx$ (1 + .26) or by $(5)^{1/3}$ = 1.70998 . . . $\approx$ (1 + .71). The factor $(3)^{1/3}$ is less convenient, and is perhaps best approximated by the fraction 10.1/7.

Higher-Order Roots

Since fourth roots can be extracted as two successive square roots, we continue on to fifth roots, say to $(48)^{1/5} = 2.16894354 \ldots$. In general, a second iteration of any technique is prohibitive, so we can explore algorithms that increase the complexity of each iteration. For an initial estimate of $a_0 = 2$, a weighted average of a_0 and $48/(2)^4$ gives $a_1 = 2.2$. Subtracting Chebyshev's term results in $a_1' = 2.16$. Three-fifthing, from Equation 8, produces from a_0 the value $2(41.6/38.4) = 2(13/12) = 2.1667 \ldots$. The complementary process of tenthing, from Equation 11, produces from a_0 the value $(48/16) \bullet (33.6/46.4) = 3(21/29) = 2.1724 \ldots$. Their weighted average yields $2.1678 \ldots$.

Another method for higher roots like this is to write the equation $N - a^p = 0$ as

$$\left(\frac{a}{a_n}\right)^p = \frac{N}{a_n^p}$$

Now, for $-a_n \ll (a - a_n) \ll a_n$, we can use the relation [27,28],

$$\left(\frac{a}{a_n}\right)^p \approx \frac{p}{q}\left(\frac{a}{a_n}\right)^q + \frac{q - p}{q}$$

to convert the equation into one of a degree that simplifies the process of solving it. Substituting, we get

$$\frac{p}{q}\left(\frac{a}{a_n}\right)^q + \frac{q - p}{q} \approx \frac{N}{a_n^p}$$

and rearranging terms,

$$a^q \approx \frac{q}{p}\frac{N}{a_n^{p-q}} + \left(1 - \frac{q}{p}\right)a_n^q$$

This can be iterated:

$$a_{n+1}^q = \frac{q}{p} \frac{N}{a_n^{p-q}} + \left(1 - \frac{q}{p}\right) a_n^q$$

If we stretch this method to the limit, we can let the new degree q be 1; then, for $p = 5$, $N = 48$ and $a_0 = 2$,

$$a_1 = (1/5) \bullet 48/(2)^4 + (4/5) \bullet 2$$

$$= 2.2$$

This is the same answer we obtained from the weighted average earlier, and indeed this relation always reduces to a weighted average if $q = 1$. (Incidentally, cascading the equation down to $q = 1$ by steps of 1 results in the same formula as above for a_1). Therefore, we can expect to do better if we reduce the order p by less. For example, we can let $q = 4$ and solve for a_1 by successive square roots:

$$a_1^4 = (4/5) \bullet (48/2) + (1/5) \bullet (2)^4 = 22.4$$

$$a_1^2 = 4.7328 \ldots$$

$$a_1 = 2.1755 \ldots$$

a procedure still not as accurate as two-fifthing or tenthing, much less their weighted average. However, since we only divide here by a_0, not by powers of a_0 as in the previous algorithms, we can stretch our capabilities of multiplication and actually use $a_1 = 2.2$ to calculate an iteration:

$$a_2^4 = (4/5) \bullet (48/2.2) + (1/5) \bullet (2.2)^4$$

Now in this case, we may recall that the pth power of 11 is the single-digit melded $(p + 1)$th row of Pascal's Triangle. The fifth row is 1,4,6,4,1, so $(2.2)^4 = 16(1.4641) = 23.4256$. Alternatively, since $(22)^2 = 484$, then we find $(484)^2 = 500 \bullet 468 + (16)^2$. Or again, we can use the rule of 25 on $(48.4)^2 = (25 - 1.6)|00 + (1.6)^2$ and remove the decimal point. In any event, we soon arrive at

$a_2^4 = 22.139665\ldots$

$a_2^2 = 4.7052806\ldots$

$a_2 = 2.169166\ldots$

our closest approximation yet to $2.1689435\ldots$.

Yet another approach for fifth roots was published by DeLagney in 1692 [3,14]:

$$(a^5 + b)^{1/5} \approx \left(\left(\frac{b}{5a} + \frac{a^4}{4}\right)^{1/2} - \frac{a^2}{4}\right)^{1/2} + \frac{a}{2}$$

For **a** = 2 and **b** = 16 (not, as you might imagine, an ideal circumstance), we find

$$(48)^{1/5} = [(1.6 + 4)^{1/2} - 1]^{1/2} + 1$$

$$= (1.3664319\ldots)^{1/2} + 1$$

$$= 2.1689448\ldots$$

which is extremely good, considering that **b** is not small compared to a^5.

Further yet, it is not wholly unreasonable at this point (or is it?) to perform this approximation with **a** = 2.2. As before, we arrive at $a^4 = 23.4256$ and therefore $a^4/4 = 5.8564$. Now $2(23.4256) = 46.8512$ and $a^5 = 46.8512 + 4.68512 = 51.53632$, giving us the result **b** = −3.53632. Then,

$$(48)^{1/5} = [(-3.53632/11 + 5.8564)^{1/2} - 1.21]^{1/2} + 1.1$$

$$= (5.5349164\ldots - 1.21)^{1/2} + 1.1$$

$$= 2.16894364\ldots \text{ compared to } 2.16894354\ldots$$

In addition to this method's higher accuracy over others, it offers very simple divisors in its terms, an important benefit for mental use. Halley generally preferred these approximations involving square roots to rational approximations (fractions whose numerators and denominators are polynomials) because ". . . manifold Experience has taught me" that square root extraction is easier than division by a large number [14].

An alternative is to use an approximation, again by Halley, that contains only one square root extraction [14]:

$$(a^p + b)^{1/p} \approx \frac{p - 2}{p - 1} a + \frac{1}{p - 1} [a^2 + 2ba^{2-p}(1 - 1/p)]^{1/2}$$

which falls directly out of a new iterative relation for finding real roots of a real polynomial equation:

$$a_{n+1} = a_n - \frac{f'(a_n)}{f''(a_n)} + \frac{[f'(a_n)^2 - 2f(a_n) \; f''(a_n)]^{1/2}}{f''(a_n)}$$

Now for **p** = 5,

$$(a^5 + b)^{1/5} \approx 3a/4 + (1/4) \bullet (a^2 + 8b/5a^3)^{1/2}$$

Repeating the above example of **a** = 2, **b** = 16, we find

$$(48)^{1/5} \approx 3 \bullet 2/4 + (1/4) \bullet (4 + 16/5)^{1/2}$$

$$= 1.5 + (2.68328 \ldots)/4$$

$$= 2.1708 \ldots$$

This is not too bad considering the reduction in effort over the formula involving nested square roots; on the other hand, the case **a** = 2.2 is prohibitive here.

You don't have to do many of these approximations, particularly for numbers far from a perfect power, before it becomes apparent that, in general, the way to extract higher-order roots is through logarithms. The conversion to and from logarithmic form is not as hard as it may seem, and we will address this subject in the next chapter.

How far can we go, then, in mentally extracting roots? At least for square roots, we can with our general method achieve a result whose accuracy depends only on our patience and care. The mathematician John Wallis (1616–1703) wrote in 1669 that "In a dark night, in bed, without pen, ink or paper or anything equivalent," he mentally extracted the square root of (in his notation)

3,00000,00000,00000,00000,00000,00000,00000,00000

and found it to be 1,73205,08075,68877,29353 to 21 digits. Two months later he wrote that he did the same for the 53-digit number

24681357910121411131516182017192122242628302325272931

and found the result to be 157103016871482805817152171 to 27 digits [2].
I think we can take this as something of a benchmark.

Bibliography

1. A. C. Aitken, "The Art of Mental Calculation; with Demonstrations," *Transactions of the Society of Engineers*, **44** (1954) pp. 295–309.
2. Steven B. Smith, *The Great Mental Calculators*, Columbia University Press, New York, 1983, pp. 123–135, 266, 331–332.
3. D. F. Bailey, "A Historical Survey of Solution by Functional Iteration," *Mathematics Magazine*, **62** (1989) pp. 155–166.
4. D. E. Smith, *History of Mathematics Vol. II: Special Topics of Elementary Mathematics*, Dover, New York, 1925, pp. 150, 605.
5. Carl N. Shuster, "Approximate Square Roots," *The Mathematics Teacher*, **45** (1952) pp. 17–18.
6. Ladis D. Kovach, "Ancient Algorithms Adapted to Modern Computers," *Mathematics Magazine*, **37** (1964) pp. 159–165.
7. Tom R. Bauerochse, "Square Roots by an Iterative Method and Its Generalization to Positive Integral Roots of Order **n**," *Mathematics Magazine*, **39** (1966) pp. 219–223.
8. George Miel, "Of Calculations Past and Present: The Archimedean Algorithm," *American Mathematical Monthly*, **90** (1983) pp. 17–35.

9. George H. Brown, "On Halley's Variation of Newton's Method," *American Mathematical Monthly,* 84 (1977) pp. 726–728.

10. J. K. Stewart, "Another Variation of Newton's Method," *American Mathematical Monthly,* 58 (1951) pp. 331–334.

11. C. T. Fike, *Computer Evaluation of Mathematical Functions,* Prentice-Hall, Englewood Cliffs, 1968, pp. 22–24, 36–37.

12. J. F. Traub, "Comparison of Iterative Methods for the Calculation of nth Roots," *Communications of the ACM,* 4 (1961) pp. 143–145.

13. Walter Gander, "On Halley's Iteration Method," *American Mathematical Monthly,* 92 (1985) pp. 131–134.

14. Harry Bateman, "Halley's Methods for Solving Equations," *American Mathematical Monthly,* 45 (1938) pp. 11–17.

15. Stewart M. Venit, "Remarks Concerning the Delta Method for Approximating Roots," *Two-Year College Mathematics Journal,* 7 (1976) pp. 1–3.

16. Graham Hoare, "Rational Approximations to $a^{1/p}$—an Investigation," *The Mathematical Gazette,* 67 (1983) pp. 223–226.

17. Christopher Bradley, "A Theorem Concerning Rational Approximations to $a^{1/p}$," *The Mathematical Gazette,* 67 (1983) pp. 226–227.

18. J. V. Uspensky, *Theory of Equations,* McGraw-Hill, New York, 1948, pp. 174–180.

19. Derrick Henry Lehmer, "A Cross-Division Process and Its Application to the Extraction of Roots," *American Mathematical Monthly,* 33 (1926) pp. 198–206.

20. J. P. Ballantine, "Note on the Multiplication of Long Decimals," *American Mathematical Monthly,* 30 (1923) pp. 68–69.

21. Wendy James and P. Jarrett, "The Generation of Square Roots on a Computer with Rapid Multiplication Compared with Division," *Mathematics of Computation,* 19 (1965) pp. 497–500.

22. Glenn James, "A Rapid Method of Approximating Arithmetic Roots," *American Mathematical Monthly,* 31 (1924) pp. 471–475.

23. Henry Laufer, "Finding the Nth Root of a Number by Iteration," *Mathematics Magazine,* 36 (1963) pp. 157–162.

24. E. M. Romer, "A Comment on Finding the Nth Root of a Number by Iteration," *Mathematics Magazine,* 36 (1963) pp. 315–316.

25. A. M. Cohen, "Approximating Square Roots and Cube Roots," *The Mathematical Gazette*, 67 (1983) pp. 221–223.

26. Preston C. Hammer, "Iterative Procedures for Taking Roots Based on Square Roots," *Mathematical Tables and other Aids to Computation*, 9 (1955) p. 68.

27. Eugene Romer, "An Extension of An Approximation for Any Positive Integral Root," *Mathematics Magazine*, 37 (1964) pp. 187–192.

28. Sylvan Burgstahler, "An Algorithm for Solving Polynomial Equations," *American Mathematical Monthly*, 93 (1986) pp. 421–430.

Logarithms and Their Inverses

It can be said without exaggeration that our modern cities with their bridges, railroads, factories, power installations, skyscrapers, in short, all our highly artificial environment, built by mankind during the last century or two, and which implies an enormous amount of numerical computations, would be impossible without the tables of logarithms.

E.G. Kogbetliantz (1968) [1]

The principles of logarithms were discovered first by Archimedes, then rediscovered and used by Iranian astronomers in the thirteenth century, and finally discovered again and published by John Napier (1550–1617) in 1614. In addition to spontaneously arising as functions in the solution of mathematical and physical differential equations, they provide us with tools for vastly simplifying arithmetic operations such as multiplication, division, powers, and roots. In fact, Napier's original intention for these functions was to ease calculations of trigonometric formulas, demonstrating their range of applications. Specifically, when nautical tables were unavailable or simply not used, the trigonometric

113

calculations needed for estimating position and time were historically done using logarithms. Slide rules were strictly based on logarithms, and many computer routines rely on them as well.

The logarithm of a number **N** to a base **B** is defined to be the value **x** such that

$$B^x = N$$

Therefore,

$$x = \log_B N$$

where the subscript **B** denotes the base of the logarithm. "Common" logarithms have a base of 10, and the notation log **N** with no subscript is usually considered, as it is here, to have this decimal base. The common logarithm **x** = log **N** has an inverse, then, given by **N** = 10^x.

A base not tied to the base of our number system, but providing a convenient, or "natural," base for logarithmic solutions to differential equations, is denoted by the letter **e**. The value of the transcendental number **e** in our base 10 arithmetic is 2.718281828 . . . , and the notation for the logarithm to base **e**, the natural logarithm, is generally given by ln **N**. The inverse of the natural logarithm **x** = ln **N** is given by the exponential function **N** = e^x.

Logarithms are useful in arithmetic calculations because they have the following properties:

$$\log (ab) = \log a + \log b$$

$$\log (a/b) = \log a - \log b$$

$$\log (a^b) = b \log a$$

$$\log (a^{1/b}) = (\log a)/b$$

These are true regardless of the base of the logarithm.

In short, logarithms reduce multiplications and divisions to additions and subtractions, and convert powers and roots to multiplications and divisions. For our purposes, their latter use is of the most benefit. To find, say, the seventh root of 13781, we could find log 13781, divide by 7, and find the answer as 10 to that power. The accuracy of the answer is limited only by the number of digits retained in the calculation. Also, it may be easier to find either log N or ln N, depending on N, but it is almost always easier to raise 10 to a power than to raise e to a power. This ultimately requires us to work with common logarithms when inverses are required.

To find a means of converting from common logarithms to natural logarithms (and back), we begin with relations that, by the definition of a function and its inverse, are given by

$$10 = e^{\ln 10}$$

$$e = 10^{\log e}$$

Substituting the second into the first relation, we have

$$10 = (10^{\log e})^{\ln 10} = 10^{\log e \ln 10}$$

Therefore, log e ln 10 = 1. For a number N given by

$$10^{\log N} = x = e^{\ln N}$$

we again substitute the relation $e = 10^{\log e}$ to get

$$10^{\log N} = 10^{\log e \ln N}$$

or,

$$\log N = \log e \ln N$$

Therefore, we arrive at log N by multiplying ln N by the constant log e, and we use the reciprocal of this constant to convert from log N to ln N. From formulas given later, we can find log e = 0.4342945 ... (or about .4343) and (1/log e) = ln 10 = 2.302585 ..., so

$$\log N \approx .4343 \ln N$$

$$\ln N \approx 2.303 \log N$$

Again, we often are not interested in finding inverse logarithms; natural logarithms appear very often in formulas requiring calculation.

In any event, the conversion of a number into logarithmic form and back is a useful and entertaining knack, and the tools for mentally doing so are the subject of this chapter.

General Logarithmic Approximations

At first glance, it may appear to be an enormous task to calculate logarithms, as it was for Napier, Briggs, and others. We see first that log 1 = 0 (a definition, actually) since $(10)^0 = 1$. Also, log 10 = 1, log 100 = 2, and so on, but intermediate values offer little hope. We can take, for example, $(10)^{1/2} = 3.1622777\ldots$, but this just gives us log $(3.1622777\ldots) = 0.5$, something akin to throwing darts at the problem.

The general procedure, and one deduced by Henry Briggs (1556–1630) in devising his tables of logarithms published in 1617 and 1624, is to use the properties of logarithms given earlier to reduce the argument of the logarithm to a value very close to 1. Then, truncating the following well-known power series provides the natural logarithm to the degree of approximation desired:

$$\ln (1 + x) = x - \frac{x^2}{2} + \frac{x^3}{3} - \frac{x^4}{4} + \ldots \qquad \text{for } -1 \leq x < 1 \qquad (14)$$

It is the cleverness we exhibit in reducing the logarithm to a value near 1 that makes calculating logarithms a most creative and engaging activity, and lightning calculators have had a deep appreciation of this [2].

A very interesting description of Napier's and Briggs' development of logarithmic tables, as well as the efforts of others later, is found in Goldstine [3]. We will consider these and other available techniques best applied to mental calculation.

Obviously, the optimum procedure is to leave x = 0, which amounts to factoring the argument into powers of ten and low primes whose logarithms are memorized. If that is not possible, we can factor a number very close to the argument and extract a value of **x** for the power series correction. To illustrate, log 1200 = log [3 • (2)^2 • 100]

$\qquad$ = log 3 + 2 • log 2 + 2

$\qquad$ ≈ .47712 + 2(.30103) + 2

$\qquad$ ≈ 3.07918

log 1211 = log [1200 • (1 + 11/1200)]

$\qquad$ = log 1200 + (.4343 . . .) • [11/1200

$\qquad$ − ½ (11/1200)^2 + . . .]

Taking only the first term of the series expansion and letting .4343 . . . become simply .43, we have

log 1211 ≈ 3.07918 + .43(11/1200)

$\qquad$ ≈ 3.08312 $\qquad$ Actual: 3.08314

If we had preferred, we could have divided by 2.302585 ≈ 2.3 instead of multiplying by .4343. Dividing by 2.3 gives log 1200 ≈ 3.08317.

Alternatively, we could have taken

log 1211 = log 1210 + log (1 + 1/1210)

since 1210 is easily factored into low primes and a power of ten and the value of **x** is smaller.

A variation on this was used by the mental calculator George Parker Bidder (1806–1878) [2]:

log (1 + x) ≈ 10^m • x • log (1 + 10^{-m}) $\quad$ for 10^m < x < 10^{m+1}

The value of **m** is simply that which makes the term 10^{m}x lie between 1 and 10. We need to know log (1 + 10^{-m}) as well:

log 1.01 = .00432 . . .

log 1.001 = .000434 . . .

log 1.0001 = .0000434 . . .

etc.

Obviously, as **m** increases, the digits of log $(1 + 10^{-m})$ approach those of log $e = 0.4343 \ldots$.
To repeat the previous example,

$$\log 1211 = \log 1200 + \log (1 + 11/1200)$$

$$\approx 3.07918 + (11/1.2) \log 1.001$$

$$\approx 3.07918 + .00398$$

$$\approx 3.08316$$

Where does this approximation come from? We know from Equation 14 that

$$\ln (1 + x) \approx x$$

$$\ln (1 + 10^{-m}) \approx 10^{-m}$$

$$\frac{\ln (1 + x)}{\ln (1 + 10^{-m})} = \frac{\log (1 + x)}{\log (1 + 10^{-m})} \approx 10^m x$$

$$\log (1 + x) \approx 10^m \bullet x \bullet \log (1 + 10^{-m})$$

Now, since **m** is chosen so that **x** and 10^{-m} are about equal, the errors in truncating their series are of the same order; therefore, this approximation is more accurate than that obtained by simply truncating the series for log $(1 + x)$.

It becomes clear that we can vastly improve our performance if we memorize the logarithms of a range of low-order primes, say, up to 11.

log 2 = .30103 . . .

log 3 = .47712 . . .

log 5 = log (10/2) = 1 − log 2

log 7 = .84510 . . .

log 11 = 1.04139 . . .

Actually, it's an intriguing pursuit to estimate these as well, and very useful if they're not memorized [4,5]. For example,

$(2)^{10}$ = 1024 ≈ 1000

so,

10 log 2 ≈ 3, or log 2 ≈ .3

Here we could really improve the estimate:

10 log 2 ≈ 3 + .4343(24/1000)

    log 2 ≈ .30104 . . .

and if we dare to include the next term in the series expansion, $−.4343(.024)^2/2$ = −.0001251 . . . , and divide by the factor 10 again,

    log 2 ≈ .3010298 . . .   Actual: .301029996 . . .

illustrating that we don't have to have a large number to arrive at a small value of **x** if we use our imagination.

    Other relations we can come up with (and improve with correction terms) include:

$$3^4 = 81 ≈ 2^3 \bullet 10$$

$$3^4 \bullet 5^3 = 10125 ≈ 10^4$$

$$7^2 = 49 \approx 10^2/2$$

$$3 \bullet 7^3 = 1029 \approx 10^3$$

$$2^4 \bullet 3^2 \bullet 7 = 1008 \approx 10^3$$

$$11^2 = 121 \approx 2^2 \bullet 3 \bullet 10$$

$$7 \bullet 11 \bullet 13 = 1001, \text{ or } \log 13 \approx 3 - \log 11 - \log 7$$

$$27 \bullet 37 = 999, \text{ or } \log 37 \approx 3 - 3 \log 3$$

The last two products we recall from the Chapter 2 discussion of divisibility (notice the result if we multiply them together!). In fact, one reason for the amount of time spent earlier on factoring numbers is the application here in calculating logarithms.

We can create many of these relations, some very complicated but precise [6]. One type of relation that is generally useful for finding the logarithm of a prime **p** is

$$p^2 = (p + 1) \bullet (p - 1) + 1$$

$$\approx (p + 1) \bullet (p - 1)$$

All prime factors of **(p + 1)** • **(p − 1)** must be less than **p**. Mermin [4] gives the following examples (there are obviously many more):

$$(3^2 \bullet 11)^2 \approx 100 \bullet 98$$

$$7^4 \approx 50 \bullet 48 = (100/2) \bullet 3 \bullet 2^4$$

$$21^2 \approx 22 \bullet 20 = 2^2 \bullet 11 \bullet 10$$

We can even use this in our example of finding log 1211. In this case, the error in dropping 1 is extremely small.

$$(1211)^2 = 1212 \cdot 1210 + 1 \approx 1212 \cdot 1210$$

$$= 12 \cdot 101 \cdot 121 \cdot 10$$

$$= 2^2 \cdot 3 \cdot 10 \cdot 11^2 \cdot 101$$

$$\log 1211 \approx \log 2 + \log 11 + \tfrac{1}{2}\,[\log 3 + \log 10 + \log 100$$

$$+ .4343(.01)]$$

$$\approx .30103 + 1.04139 + \tfrac{1}{2}\,(.47712 + 1 + 2 + .00434)$$

$$\approx 3.08315$$

Rounding errors produced the error in the last digit.

Neighboring Value Relations

Another form of relation for the natural logarithm $\ln N$ (which, as earlier, is easily converted to the common logarithm $\log N$) uses a variable transformation [1,7]:

$$u = \frac{N - 1}{N + 1} \qquad \text{or} \qquad N = \frac{1 + u}{1 - u}$$

Then, from Equation 14,

$$\ln N = 2(u + u^3/3 + u^5/5 + \ldots) \tag{15}$$

where we have now eliminated the even terms in the expansion. However, this is mostly useful for N near 1, as the series converges very slowly otherwise.

A much better approach in general is to take Equation 15 and replace N with the expression $(N + 1)/N$. Then u becomes $1/(2N + 1)$ and Equation 15 reduces to the very nice result:

$$\ln (N + 1) = \ln N + \frac{2}{2N + 1}$$

$$\times \left[1 + \frac{1}{3(2N + 1)} + \frac{1}{5(2N + 1)^4} + \dots \right] \quad (16)$$

This converges very rapidly for larger values of **N**.

Notice that if we take one term of the earlier series expansion (Equation 14), we find

$$\ln (N + 1) = \ln [N(1 + 1/N)]$$

$$= \ln N + \ln (1 + 1/N)$$

$$\approx \ln N + 1/N$$

The new series (Equation 16) produces a more accurate value when the first term is taken, and converges more rapidly:

$$\ln (N + 1) \approx \ln N + \frac{2}{2N + 1}$$

Therefore, setting the conversion factor .4343 . . . to simply .43 for this small second term,

$$\log 1211 \approx \log 1210 + .43(2/2423)$$

but,

$$\log 1210 = 2 \log 11 + \log 10 = 3.08279 \dots$$

so,

$$\log 1211 \approx 3.08279 + .00036$$

$$\approx 3.08315$$

Obviously, more digits are needed here to show the greater accuracy, a pleasant situation after all. Of course, we are considering here precision to the fifth decimal place; in reality, we can reduce this precision if we want to simplify the calculations.

We can also replace N in Equation 15 by $(N - 1)/N$, giving us a relation for $\ln (N - 1)$:

$$\ln (N - 1) = \ln N - \frac{2}{2N - 1}$$

$$\times \left[1 + \frac{1}{3(2N - 1)} + \frac{1}{5(2N - 1)^4} + \cdots \right]$$

This is not as useful for finding log 1211, as 1212 does not factor quite as nicely as 1210 does.

In general, if a is a positive or negative number,

$$\ln (N + a) = \ln N - \frac{2a}{2N + a}$$

$$\times \left[1 + \frac{1}{3(2N + a)} + \frac{1}{5(2N + a)^4} + \cdots \right]$$

Intermediate Value Relations

There is also a nice formula due to Halley for finding the logarithm of a number N equidistant between two numbers a and b whose logarithms are easier to calculate [3]. For $N = \frac{1}{2}(a + b)$,

$$\log \frac{(ab)^{1/2}}{N} = \log \frac{(ab)^{1/2}}{\frac{1}{2}(a + b)}$$

$$= \frac{1}{2} \log \frac{4ab}{(a + b)^2}$$

$$= \frac{1}{2} \log \left[1 - \frac{(b - a)^2}{(a + b)^2} \right]$$

or, from Equation 14,

$$\log (ab)^{1/2} - \log N = \tfrac{1}{2} (.4343 \ldots)$$

$$\bullet \left[\frac{(b - a)^2}{(a + b)^2} - \tfrac{1}{2} \frac{(b - a)^4}{(a + b)^4} + \ldots \right]$$

For (b – a) small compared to (a + b), this relation converges very fast due to the squaring of the denominator. Retaining only the first term of the expansion, we arrive at

$$\log N \approx \tfrac{1}{2} \left[\log a + \log b + .4343 \frac{(b - a)^2}{(a + b)^2} \right] \tag{17}$$

Now for b – a = 2, we can derive an amazing formula in the following manner:

$$\frac{4ab}{(a + b)^2} = \frac{4a(a + 2)}{[a + (a + 2)]^2}$$

$$= \frac{2a^2 + 4a}{2a^2 + 4a + 2}$$

$$= \left[\frac{(2a^2 + 4a + 1) + 1}{(2a^2 + 4a + 1) - 1} \right]^{-1}$$

$$= \left[\frac{1 + 1/(2a^2 + 4a + 1)}{1 - 1/(2a^2 + 4a + 1)} \right]^{-1}$$

If we make the transformation

$$y^2 = 2a^2 + 4a + 1$$

(where the square of y is denoted to indicate the order of magnitude of the result), then

$$- \log \frac{(ab)^{1/2}}{N} = - \frac{1}{2} \log \frac{1 + 1/y^2}{1 - 1/y^2}$$

or, from Equation 15,

$$- \log \frac{(ab)^{1/2}}{N} = (.4343\ldots) \bullet \left[\frac{1}{y^2} + \frac{1}{3y^6} + \frac{1}{5y^{10}} + \ldots \right]$$

It is difficult, I think, to appreciate the rate of convergence of this expression without an example. Halley provides an example of finding log 23:

$$y^2 = 1057$$

$$- \log \frac{(22 \bullet 24)^{1/2}}{23} = (.4343\ldots) \bullet \left[\frac{1}{1057} + \frac{1}{3542796579} + \ldots \right]$$

Even for small numbers, then, the second and later terms are extremely negligible. Continuing,

$$\log 23 \approx \frac{1}{2} (\log 22 + \log 24) + .43/1057$$

$$\log 22 = \log 2 + \log 11 = 1.34242\ldots$$

$$\log 24 = 3 \log 2 + \log 3 = 1.38021\ldots$$

$$\text{average} = 1.36132\ldots$$

$$\log 23 \approx 1.36132 + .00041$$

$$\approx 1.36173$$

This result is accurate to the last digit, which is all the accuracy we were retaining in the calculation. The formula is obviously capable of extreme accuracy, however, and for those who anticipate pursuing it, a convenient multiplier to replace .43 in approximating .4342945 . . . is given by the fraction 43/99 = .434343 . . . (the value 1/2.3 = .43478 . . .). The best alternative we have found so far in calculating the logarithm of a relatively low prime number such as this is:

$$(23)^2 = 22 \bullet 24 + 1 \approx 22 \bullet 24$$

$$\log 23 \approx \tfrac{1}{2} (\log 22 + \log 24)$$

which is seen as simply the first term of the last result.

Halley's method does require division by y^2 and multiplication by .4343 . . . , although we only kept two digits in these operations. However, we can eliminate even these nuisances, given that we know the logarithms of the neighboring numbers, at the cost of some of this extreme accuracy [3]. This relation is due to the ubiquitous Newton and for practical purposes the reduction in accuracy is not important.

Newton defined for $a = N - x$ and $b = N + x$:

$$d = \tfrac{1}{2} (\log b - \log a)$$

Then,

$$2d = \log \frac{N + x}{N - x}$$

$$= \log \frac{1 + x/N}{1 - x/N}$$

and from Equation 15,

$$2d = \frac{x}{N} + \frac{x^3}{3N^3} + \frac{x^5}{5N^5} + \ldots$$

Also, the difference $(\log N - \log a)$ can be denoted as g:

$$g = \log \frac{N}{N - x} = - \log (1 - x/N)$$

From Equation 14,

$$g = \frac{x}{N} + \frac{x^2}{2N^2} + \frac{x^3}{3N^3} + \ldots$$

Therefore,

$$\frac{g}{2d} = \frac{\dfrac{x}{N} + \dfrac{x^2}{2N^2} + \dfrac{x^3}{3N^3} + \ldots}{\dfrac{x}{N} + \dfrac{x^3}{3N^3} + \dfrac{x^5}{5N^5} + \ldots}$$

Dividing through, we arrive at

$$g = d + \frac{\frac{1}{2}dx}{N} + \frac{(1/12)\ dx^3}{N^3} + \ldots$$

or,

$$g \approx d + \frac{\frac{1}{2}dx}{N}$$

Since **g** is the amount to be added to log **a** and **d** = ½ (log **b** − log **a**), we can rewrite this as:

$$\log N \approx \tfrac{1}{2}(\log a + \log b) + \frac{\frac{1}{2}dx}{N} \tag{18}$$

As **d** implicitly contains the constant .4343 . . . in finding the difference between common logarithms, we are rid of this multiplication. In addition, we divide by a number **N**, not by the much larger value $y^2 = 2a^2 + 4a + 1$ of Halley's method. It is also easier than Equation 17 for **x** > 1.

Returning to our previous example for log 23 with **x** = 1:

$$\log 23 \approx \tfrac{1}{2} \left(\log 22 + \log 24\right) + \frac{\tfrac{1}{2}d \cdot 1}{23}$$

$$\log 22 = \log 2 + \log 11 = 1.34242\ldots$$

$$\log 24 = 3 \log 2 + \log 3 = 1.38021\ldots$$

$$\text{average} = 1.36132\ldots$$

$$d = .018895\ldots$$

$$\log 23 \approx 1.36132 + .00945/23$$

$$\approx 1.36173$$

The result is identical to Halley's method to the accuracy retained throughout the calculation. Notice that we can simply subtract log 22 from the average to find **d**, since $\tfrac{1}{2}$ (log **a** + log **b**) – log **a** = $\tfrac{1}{2}$ (log **b** – log **a**). Now if we actually knew log 22 and log 23 to extreme accuracy (and multiplied by .4342945 . . . in Halley's method), we would find these results:

Halley's Method: log 23 = 1.36172783590 . . .

Newton's Method: log 23 = 1.36172770649 . . .

Actual Value: log 23 = 1.36172783602 . . .

The impressive accuracy of Newton's method for **x** = 1 leads us to try log 23 for **x** = 2. While perhaps necessary in general for some numbers **N**, the case **x** = 2 is actually a little easier for log 23 as well if log 7 is known.

$$\log 23 \approx \tfrac{1}{2} \left(\log 21 + \log 25\right) + \frac{\tfrac{1}{2}d \cdot 2}{23}$$

$$\log 21 = \log 3 + \log 7 = 1.322219\ldots$$

$$\log 25 = 2 \log 5 = 1.397940\ldots$$

average = 1.360080 . . .

d = .03786 . . .

log 23 ≈ 1.360080 + .03786/23

≈ 1.36173

Again, this is accurate to the number of digits retained. More exact values would give log 23 = 1.361725754 . . . .

In short, Newton's method gives highly accurate results for reasonable values of x without the more difficult multiplication and division of Halley's method.

This leads us naturally to consider another more general interpolation technique. For a known set of values $f(x_0)$, $f(x_1)$, . . . , $f(x_n)$ located near or around the unknown value $f(x)$, where x_0, x_1, . . . , x_n are not necessarily equally spaced, the most straightforward technique for mental calculation of $f(x)$ is through Lagrange's formula [3]:

$$f(x) \approx \sum_{k=0}^{n} \frac{\prod_{k \neq m} (x - x_m)}{\prod_{k \neq m} (x_k - x_m)} f(x_k)$$

where again the Greek letter sigma here represents the sum of terms for k = 0 to n, and the Greek letter pi represents the product of all terms except for k = m.

Let us consider the calculation of log 13 = 1.1139434 . . . . Since log 11, log 12, log 14 and log 15 may be easily generated from factors (assuming the logarithms of primes ≤ 11 are memorized), we would expect a better result than Newton's formula (Equation 18), which involves just log 12 and log 14.

For x_k of this spacing, Lagrange's formula reduces to:

$$\log 13 = -\frac{1}{6} \log 11 + \frac{2}{3} \log 12 + \frac{2}{3} \log 14 - \frac{1}{6} \log 15$$

log 11 = 1.04139 . . .

$$\log 12 = 2 \log 2 + \log 3 = 1.07918\ldots$$

$$\log 14 = \log 2 + \log 7 = 1.14613\ldots$$

$$\log 15 = \log 3 + (1 - \log 2) = 1.17609\ldots$$

$$\log 13 \approx (1/6) \cdot [-(1.04139\ldots) + 4(1.07918\ldots)$$

$$+ 4(1.14613\ldots) - (1.17609\ldots)]$$

$$\approx 1.1139589\ldots \qquad \text{Actual value: } 1.1139434\ldots$$

Newton's formula for **x** = 1 gives

$$\log 13 \approx \tfrac{1}{2}\,(\log 12 + \log 14) + \frac{\tfrac{1}{2}d \cdot 1}{13}$$

$$\log 12 = 1.07918\ldots$$

$$\log 14 = 1.14613\ldots$$

$$\text{average} = 1.11265\ldots$$

$$d = .03347\ldots$$

$$\log 13 \approx 1.11265\ldots + (.003347\ldots)/26$$

$$\approx 1.1139421\ldots$$

We find here that Newton's formula is in fact a superior approach to the standard Lagrange interpolation performed on twice as many data points!

An Iterative Relation

One other approach to finding logarithms involves an iterative method known as Borchardt's Algorithm, accelerated by a technique called Richardson extrapolation [8,9]. While this method involves extracting a square root and dividing by a multidigit number, I find it impossible to exclude because of its extreme accuracy and the minimal memorization required (log 2 and the formula itself). The square root is manageable by the techniques of Chapter 3; the division may be performed by the cross division technique described in Chapter 2 if desired. Perhaps in a pinch this provides a good pencil and paper approximation.

The iterative relation, which we will truncate very early, is given for $N > 0$ and $n = 0,1,2,\ldots$ as

$$a_0 = \tfrac{1}{2}\,(1 + N)$$

$$g_0 = N^{1/2}$$

$$a_{n+1} = \tfrac{1}{2}\,(a_n + g_n)$$

$$g_{n+1} = (a_{n+1} \bullet g_n)^{1/2}$$

The acceleration is achieved by the relations:

$$d(0,n) = a_n$$

$$d(k,n) = \frac{d(k - 1,n) - 2^{-2k} \bullet d(k - 1,n - 1)}{1 - 2^{-2k}}$$

for $k = 1,2,3,\ldots,n.$
Finally,

$$\ln N \approx \frac{N - 1}{d(n,n)}$$

This seems incomprehensible, but we will only keep terms through $d(1,1)$:

$$d(0,0) = a_0 = \tfrac{1}{2}\,(1 + N)$$

$$d(0,1) = a_1 = \tfrac{1}{2}\,(a_0 + g_0) = \tfrac{1}{2}\,[\tfrac{1}{2}\,(1 + N) + N^{1/2}]$$

$$d(1,1) = \frac{d(0,1) - 2^{-2} \cdot d(0,0)}{1 - 2^{-2}}$$

$$= \frac{N + 1 + 4N^{1/2}}{6}$$

and we end up with the formula,

$$\ln N \approx \frac{6(N - 1)}{N + 1 + 4N^{1/2}} \qquad (19)$$

To use this formula effectively, we need to reduce the range of the argument N by extracting powers of 10 and 2 until $1/(2)^{1/2} \leq N' \leq (2)^{1/2}$. This technique of domain reduction is crucial to many computer routines using rational or polynomial approximations to functions. Since $N' = 10^p \cdot 2^m \cdot N$, then $\log N = p + m \log 2 + (.4343 \dots) \cdot \ln N'$. Of course, the algorithm when applied in computers only extracts powers of 2, as these are fast bit-shifting operations.

A plot showing the absolute error in $\ln N'$ over its reduced range is given in Figure 1. The accuracy is astonishing and does not require memorization of any constant other than $\log 2 = .3010300 \dots$ (which is easily multiplied by a small integer m) and $\log e = .4342945 \dots$.

Let's find $\log 23$:

$$\log 23 = \log (10^1 \cdot 2^1 \cdot 1.15)$$

From the methods given earlier for extracting square roots, we find $(1.15)^{1/2} = 1.0723805 \dots$. Then,

$$\log 1.15 \approx (.4343) \frac{6(.15)}{1.15 + 1 + 4.2895221}$$

$$\approx \frac{.39087}{6.4395221}$$

$$\approx .0606978 \dots$$

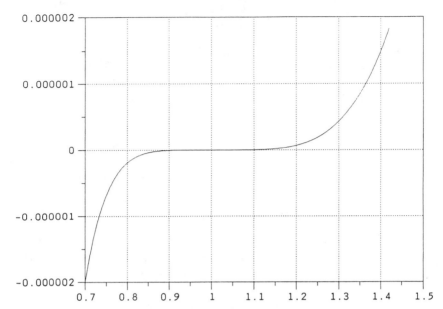

Figure 1. Absolute error of the logarithmic approximation (Equation 19) vs. N.

$$\log 23 \approx 1 + .3010300 + .0606978$$

$$\approx 1.3617278 \qquad \text{Actual value: } 1.3617278 \ldots$$

While log 23 is best taken using other methods in this chapter, this example serves to illustrate the execution and accuracy of the technique.

Approximate Logarithmic Inverses

The techniques of the previous sections can produce excellent approximations to logarithms of a number, but they provide no direct means of finding the inverses, or antilogarithms. Here we will consider this inverse as 10^x. We should realize that e^x can be calculated as $10^{(.4343\cdots)x}$; the latter is much easier to compute.

A more systematic procedure for finding logarithms can provide in tandem a procedure for finding 10^x. One method of this sort is described by Feynman [10], based on Briggs' original work. We first construct Table 7 for 2^nth roots of 10.

Feynman extends the table to the power 1/1024, but I have truncated it in an attempt to balance the required memorization

Table 7
2ⁿth Roots of 10

Power	d = Fractional Part of 64	$10^{d/64}$
1/2	32	3.16228. . .
1/4	16	1.77828. . .
1/8	8	1.33352. . .
1/16	4	1.15478. . .
1/32	2	1.07461. . .
1/64	1	1.03663. . .

and the desired accuracy. In addition, convenient fractions representing the right-hand column involve larger integers as the numbers approach 1. The following discussion is valid for any length of the table.

Notice that as the right-hand column progresses toward 1, the decimal part of the successive square roots approach that obtained by simply halving the decimal parts of the preceding entry. This is because, from the binomial series,

$$(1 + x)^{1/2} = 1 + \frac{x}{2} - \frac{x^2}{8} + \ldots$$

By computing the first 27 roots of 10 to fourteen places, Briggs was able by a more involved process described by Goldstine [3] to derive the next 27 without loss of precision.

For small **d**, we can use the relations

$$e^x = 1 + x + \frac{x^2}{2!} + \frac{x^3}{3!} + \ldots$$

$$10^x = e^{(2.303\ldots)x}$$

to find that

$$10^d \approx 1 + 2.3d \tag{20}$$

The factorial "**n**!" signifies the product of all integers between **n** and 1, inclusive (e.g., 2! = 2 • 1, 3! = 3 • 2 • 1, and so forth). The general procedure for calculating log **N**, then, is to first extract powers of 10, say 10^p, until **N** < 10. Then values of 10^d corresponding to d_1, d_2, . . . are divided out until the absolute value of **N** is less than $10^{1/64}$. Then the final term d_n can be estimated from Equation 20. Finally, since we know that

$$N = 10^p \bullet 10^{(d_1 + d_2 + \ldots + d_n)/64}$$

then

$$\log N = p + (d_1 + d_2 + \ldots + d_n)/64$$

For example, for **a** = 1211, we extract 10^3 to reduce **N** to 1.211. Then, from Table 7, d_1 = 4 provides the highest $10^{d/64}$ less than **N**, so we divide by 1.15478:

$$d_1 = 4: \frac{1.211}{1.15478} = 1.04868$$

Continuing,

$$d_2 = 1: \frac{1.04868}{1.03663} = 1.01162$$

Now we estimate d_3:

$$d_3 \approx \frac{1 - 1.01162}{2.30} = .00505$$

Then,

$$\log 1211 \approx 3 + (4 + 1)/64 + .00505$$

$$\approx 3.08318 \qquad \text{Actual value: } 3.08314 \ldots$$

Now this seems rather complicated, and it is when compared to our earlier methods. The division by 2^nth roots of 10 is in practice prohibitive. However, by using the method given in Appendix A, we can easily arrive at convenient fractions representing these values, easing the calculations. The rational approximations given in Table 8 are judgement calls of those giving reasonable accuracy and offering small integers with good factorability for simplifying calculations.

Now the calculations become a series of simpler multiplications and divisions. As it happens, we picked out the two most difficult approximations, but the calculation is manageable. We need only carry four decimal places through the calculation since the rational approximations are not extremely accurate.

$$d_1 = 4: 1.211(84/97) = 101.72/97 = 1.0487$$

$$d_2 = 1: 1.0487(27/28) = (1.0487/28) \cdot 9 \cdot 3 = 1.0112$$

$$d_3 = .0112/2.30 = .0049$$

$$\log 1211 \approx 3 + (4 + 1)/64 + .0049 \approx 3.0830$$

which suffers some from the approximations.

At any rate, the procedure is complicated for finding logarithms and requires some memorization. I present it solely because the inverse of this method provides a means of finding 10^x, which is generally a more difficult task than finding log x.

Table 8
Rational Approximations to 2^nth Roots of 10

d	$10^{d/64}$	Rational Approximation	Error
32	3.16228	253/80	$2 \cdot 10^{-4}$
16	1.77828	16/9	$5 \cdot 10^{-4}$
8	1.33352	4/3	$1 \cdot 10^{-4}$
4	1.15478	$97/84 = 97/(3 \cdot 4 \cdot 7)$	$2 \cdot 10^{-5}$
2	1.07461	43/40	$4 \cdot 10^{-4}$
1	1.03663	$28/27 = (4 \cdot 7)/(3)^3$	$4 \cdot 10^{-4}$

To illustrate this, let us reverse the problem and calculate 10^x for $x = 3.08314$. First, we extract the integer portion:

$$10^{3.08314} = 10^3 \bullet 10^{.08314}$$

Then we extract inverse powers of 2 (1/2, 1/4, 1/8, etc.) until we reach a value less than 1/64. Unless these fractions are memorized or calculated on the run, it may be best if possible to multiply the argument by 64:

$$(.08314)(64) \approx 5.3210$$

Now $5 = 4 + 1$ and $10^{.3210/64} \approx 1 + 2.30(.32)/64$, giving

$$10^{3.08314} = 10^3 \bullet (10^{(4+1)/64)} \bullet 10^{.3210/64}$$

$$\approx 10^3 \bullet (97/84) \bullet (28/27) \bullet (1.0115)$$

$$\approx 10^3 \bullet (97/81) \bullet (1.0115)$$

$$\approx 1211 \qquad \text{to four digits}$$

Another version of this general method was given by Bemer in 1958 for use in early decimal computers [11]. The idea here for finding logarithms is to first extract powers of 10 until N is *less* than one. Then, N is multiplied by a series of simple numbers until N is just greater (or less) than 1, at which point the formula for $\ln(1 + x)$ given in Equation 14 is invoked. Bemer uses the multipliers shown in Table 9, based on the first digit following the decimal point in the current value of N (other multipliers may be found in the work of Camp [12]).

Here the multipliers are simply obtained as the highest two-digit number that, when multiplied by the maximum value in the range, will result in a new value of $N \leq 1.1$. For example, the range from .1 to .2 would have a maximum value of .2, so the multiplier is $1.1/.2 = 5.5$. A value of N that will lie between 1.0 and 1.1 will be reached in at most three multiplications. The series for $\ln(1 + x)$ is then taken to the desired accuracy.

For our purposes, it is probably easier to directly use the multipliers $1.1/.2$, etc., as shown in Table 10.

Table 9
Multipliers in Bemer's Method for Logarithms

N to One Digit	Multiplier
.1	5.5
.2	3.6
.3	2.7
.4	2.2
.5	1.8
.6	1.5
.7	1.3
.8	1.2
.9	1.1

Table 10
Multipliers in Our Method for Logarithms

N to One Digit	Multiplier	Log (Multiplier)
.1	11/2	log 11 − log 2 = .7404
.2	11/3	log 11 − log 3 = .5643
.3	11/4	log 11 − log 4 = .4393
.4	11/5	log 11 − log 5 = .3424
.5	11/6	log 11 − log 6 = .2632
.6	11/7	log 11 − log 7 = .1963
.7	11/8	log 11 − log 8 = .1383
.8	11/9	log 11 − log 9 = .0872
.9	11/10	log 11 − log 10 = .0414

Again, we find log 1211:

log 1211 = 4 + log .1211

.1211(11/2) = .66605

.66605(11/7) = 1.0466

log 1211 ≈ 4 − .7404 − .1963 + .43(.0466)

≈ 3.0833

Of course, greater accuracy can be obtained by using more digits in the logarithms and more accuracy in the series expansion. Actually, we could have noticed that the intermediate value .66605 of N can be brought very close indeed to 1 if multiplied by 1.5, a logarithm easily obtained from those of low primes. It pays to be flexible.

Finding 10^x with this method parallels the method using even roots of 10. Powers of 10 are extracted from the number N until $N < 1$. Then the logarithms of the multipliers are subtracted until N is very near 1. If we do not care to explicitly memorize these logarithms as unique numbers, we can in each step subtract log 11 = 1.04139 and add the logarithm of a single-digit number (which we should be able to quickly obtain), leaving the result near 1.

The procedure continues as before:

$$10^{3.08314} = 10^3 \cdot 10^{.08314}$$

$$= 10^3 \cdot (11/9) \cdot 10^{-.0041}$$

From Equation 20,

$$10^{-.0041} \approx 1 + 2.3(-.0041) \approx .9906$$

giving, to four digits,

$$10^{3.08314} \approx 1211$$

Now let's try another example, $10^{1.67210} = 47$:

$$10^{1.67210} = 10^1 \cdot 10^{.67210}$$

$$= 10^1 \cdot (11/3) \cdot 10^{.1078}$$

$$= 10^1 \cdot (11/3) \cdot (11/9) \cdot 10^{.0206} \tag{21}$$

Again,

$$10^{.0206} \approx 1 + 2.3(.0206) = 1.0474$$

and we arrive at

$$10^{1.67210} \approx 46.94$$

Once again, greater accuracy is possible with more work. Given that log $(11/10) = .0414$, which can actually be added *or* subtracted, we ended up within 1 part in 10,000 of the worst (i.e., maximum) power of 10 we could have ($\pm.0207$). Therefore, we know we can only improve our accuracy if we choose, say, 11/4 as the first multiplier instead of the prescribed 11/3:

$$10^{1.67210} = 10^1 \bullet 10^{.6721}$$

$$= 10^1 \bullet (11/4) \bullet 10^{.2328}$$

$$= 10^1 \bullet (11/4) \bullet (11/7) \bullet 10^{.0365}$$

$$= 10^1 \bullet (11/4) \bullet (11/7) \bullet 10^{-.0049}$$

$$\approx 10^1 \bullet (11/4) \bullet (11/7) \bullet (.9887)$$

$$\approx 47.00$$

We can work out situations where the exponent of 10 ends up relatively large, say of a magnitude greater than .005. These cases amount to $10^{(a+b)}$, where $a = .02, .01, -.01,$ or $-.02$ and $b \leq .005$. Consider the case $a = .02$:

$$10^{.02} = 1.04713$$

$$1 + 2.3(.02) = \underline{1.04600}$$

$$\text{difference} = .00113$$

Then,

$$10^{(.02+b)} = 10^{.02} \bullet 10^b$$

$$\approx [1 + 2.3(.02) + .00113] \bullet (1 + 2.3b)$$

$$\approx 1 + 2.3(.02 + b) + .1b + .000113$$

Also,

$$10^{-(.02+b)} \approx 1 - 2.3(.02 + b) + .1b + .00099$$

Therefore, we will significantly improve our approximation of $10^{\pm(a+b)}$ if we always *add* to the prescribed quantity $1 \pm 2.3(a + b)$ the term $(cb + d)$, where **c** and **d** are given in Table 11.

This allows us to achieve greater accuracy from our earlier intermediate equation (Equation 21) without much additional work. Now while we could memorize $10^{.02}, \ldots, 10^{-.02}$ and directly extract these multipliers as needed, I think this is a more difficult task of memorization. More importantly, this would leave us with two multidigit numbers to multiply in the final result (10^a and 10^b) rather than one.

We arrived earlier at Equation 21:

$$10^{1.67210} = 10^1 \bullet (11/3) \bullet (11/9) \bullet 10^{.0206}$$

We now have:

$$10^{.0206} \approx 1 + 2.3(.0206) + .1(.0006) + .00113$$

$$\approx 1.0486$$

Table 11
Correction Values for $10^{\pm(a+b)}$

Sign	a	c	d
+	.02	.1	.00113
+	.01	.1/2	.00029
−	.01	.1/2	.00024
−	.02	.1	.00099

$$10^{1.67210} \approx 10^1 \cdot (11/3) \cdot (11/9) \cdot (1.0486)$$

$$\approx 46.99$$

We were actually limited by the four-place precision we retained throughout the calculation. The example given in the next section maintains five digits throughout.

An Example Problem

To demonstrate the use of logarithms in extracting higher-order roots, let's return to the mental calculation mentioned at the beginning of this chapter, the seventh root of 13781. I picked the number 13781 from a table of prime numbers and made every effort to avoid one offering special qualities for simplifying the logarithmic conversions. This is actually somewhat of an effort as the overwhelming majority of numbers have some sort of unique quality, such as being located near a number that is easily factored.

At any rate, we must first find log 13781. Personal bias leads me to the following approach:

$$\log 13781 = \log 14000 + \log (1 - 219/14000)$$

$$\log 14000 = 3 + \log 2 + \log 7$$

$$= 3 + .30103 + .84510$$

$$= 4.14613$$

Because 219/14000 is not really very small, we need to retain two terms in Equation 14, although the second can be calculated to very low precision.

$$\log (1 - 219/14000) \approx \frac{1}{2.3} \left[-\frac{219}{14000} - \frac{1}{2} \left(\frac{219}{14000} \right)^2 \right]$$

$$219/14000 = .01564$$

$$\tfrac{1}{2} (.01564)^2 \approx \tfrac{1}{2} (15)(16) \cdot 10^{-6} = 12 \cdot 10^{-5}$$

$\log (1 - 219/14000) \approx (-.01576)/2.3 = -.00685$

Therefore,

$\log 13781 \approx 4.13928$

$(1/7) \log 13781 \approx .59133$

Notice that the order of the root is almost inconsequential here. We now need the antilogarithm of this result. Using Bemer's method and retaining logarithms of the multipliers to five places, we find:

$\log 11 - \log 3 = .56427$

$10^{.59133} = (11/3) \cdot 10^{.02706}$

$\log 11 - \log 10 = .04139$

$10^{.59133} = (11/3) \cdot (11/10) \cdot 10^{-.01433}$

Now, from Table 11, which we memorized if we desire extreme accuracy,

$10^{-.01433} \approx 1 + 2.3(-.01433) + (.1/2)(.00433) + .00024$

$\approx .96750$

which yields

$10^{.59133} \approx (11/3) \cdot (11/10) \cdot (.96750)$

≈ 3.90225

compared to the actual seventh root of 13781, 3.90235 . . . .
There are many other ways, of course, to determine log 13781; upon reflection, I think a number of them will become apparent. Again, most numbers can be calculated without the second term in Equation 14 and possibly without the corrections given in Table 11.

Since the number of significant digits of a logarithm is the same as that of the number whose logarithm is taken, we need only consider five digits of the number if a five-digit result is desired. The value log 1378131, for example, may be represented as (2 + log 13781) to this accuracy.

Bibliography

1. E. G. Kogbetliantz, *Fundamentals of Mathematics from an Advanced Viewpoint Vol. II: Algebra and Analysis: Determinants–Equations–Logarithms–Limits*, Gordon and Breach, New York, 1968, pp. 470–490.
2. Steven B. Smith, *The Great Mental Calculators*, Columbia University Press, New York, 1983, pp. 150–155.
3. Herman H. Goldstine, *A History of Numerical Analysis From the 16th Through the 19th Century*, Springer-Verlag, New York, 1977, pp. 1–62, 70–71.
4. N. David Mermin, "Logarithms!," *American Journal of Physics*, 46 (1978) pp. 101–105.
5. William R. Ransom, "Elementary Calculation of Logarithms," *The Mathematics Teacher*, 47 (1954) pp. 115–116.
6. Albert A. Bennett, "Note on the Computation of Logarithms," *American Mathematical Monthly*, 28 (1921) pp. 130–131.
7. James C. Kirby, "An Efficient Logarithm Algorithm for Calculators," *College Mathematics Journal*, 19 (1988) pp. 257–260.
8. B. C. Carlson, "An Algorithm for Computing Logarithms and Arctangents," *Mathematics of Computation*, 26 (1972) pp. 543–549.
9. George Miel, "Of Calculations Past and Present: The Archimedean Algorithm," *American Mathematical Monthly*, 90 (1983) pp. 17-35.
10. Richard P. Feynman, *The Feynman Lectures in Physics Vol. I*, Addison-Wesley, Reading, 1963, section 22-4.
11. R. W. Bemer, "A Subroutine Method for Calculating Logarithms," *Communications of the Association for Computing Machinery*, 1 (1958) pp. 5–7.
12. C. C. Camp, "Logarithms of Large Numbers," *American Mathematical Monthly*, 35 (1928) pp. 547–551.

Trigonometric Functions and Their Inverses

Although this may seem a paradox, all exact science is dominated by the idea of approximation.

Bertrand Russell [1]

Trigonometric functions offer unique challenges to us in our attempts to provide convenient techniques for mental calculation. For one thing, their derivatives yield other trigonometric functions, so efforts to use approximations based on derivatives (such as the Newton-Raphson method) are generally fruitless. The orthogonality of the sine and cosine functions, which allows us to represent any function as a series of sine and cosine terms, correspondingly makes it difficult to represent them with convenient nontrigonometric functions. In addition, arithmetic operations such as sin (a + b) or (sin a + sin b) do not lend themselves well to simplification. Further, the values of at least the sine and cosine functions lie in the range from –1 to 1, sharply reducing the validity of deleting higher-order divisions or truncating power series. The tangent function spans the other extreme, from

−∞ to +∞. Finally, the radian unit of angle measure (in which the functions are most naturally and simply expressed in relations) spans for the first 0° to 90° quadrant an almost equally maddening range of 0 to 1.57.

Despite these difficulties, we will discuss here some methods of use in reckoning the basic trigonometric functions sin **x**, cos **x**, and tan **x**, as well as their inverses arcsin **x**, arccos **x**, and arctan **x**. Only the first quadrant is considered, as trigonometric values in other quadrants are easily deduced as sign changes from those in the first quadrant.

Sine and Cosine Functions

We may approach the sine function by utilizing the familiar power series:

$$\sin x = x - \frac{x^3}{3!} + \frac{x^5}{5!} - \ldots$$

where again the factorial function **n**! represents the product of all integers between **n** and 1, inclusive.

We can truncate this series, using "relaxed" coefficients to yield less overall error in this formula [2]:

$$\sin x \approx .99989x - .16596x^3 + .00760x^5$$

Now suppose we know the sine of an angle **a** in degrees and we wish to find the sine of an angle **d** a small number of degrees **b** from **a**. We can then rewrite the last relation for sin (**a** + **b**), where the radian equivalent **x** to (**a** + **b**) is given by π(**a** + **b**)/180. The Greek letter pi is the famous constant of proportionality between the circumference and the diameter of a circle, and equals 3.14159265 . . . . I assume throughout this chapter that we work in degrees instead of radians, as this occurs an overwhelming portion of the time in practice. If a calculation in radians does arise, we can convert the argument to degrees by multiplying it by 180/π, a quantity conveniently approximated by the fraction 401/7, acquired by the means detailed in Appendix A.

To continue, we arrive at

$$\sin(a + b) = .017451(a + b) - 8.8234 \cdot 10^{-7}(a + b)^3$$
$$+ 1.23 \cdot 10^{-11}(a + b)^5$$

We can multiply this out, extract the approximation for sin **a** from the right side and drop higher-order terms in **b** as negligible. Multiplying through by 1000 to ease calculations then yields the approximation,

$$1000 \sin d \approx 1000 \sin a + \frac{b}{10}\left(174 - \frac{ad}{40}\right) \qquad (22)$$

where **d** = **a** + **b**.

This formula is arranged to simplify the mental computation and is actually far easier to calculate than it first appears. It has been very useful to me, and it represents my best attempt at a reasonably convenient approximation.

How good is it? The jagged curve plotted in Figure 2 represents the absolute error curve, or the quantity (approximation – function) for this relation over the first quadrant. This curve assumes that sin **a** is known for all angles that are a multiple of 10°, yielding –5° ≤ **b** ≤ 5°.

Looking at the jagged curve, we can see that for angles **d** through 54°, represented by **a** = 50° and **b** = 4°, the approximation is accurate to three (and usually four) decimal places. Therefore, we can use this formula in the range 0° ≤ **d** ≤ 54° if we memorize the following values:

sin 0° = 0

sin 10° = .1736

sin 20° = .3420

sin 30° = .5

sin 40° = .6428

sin 50° = .7660

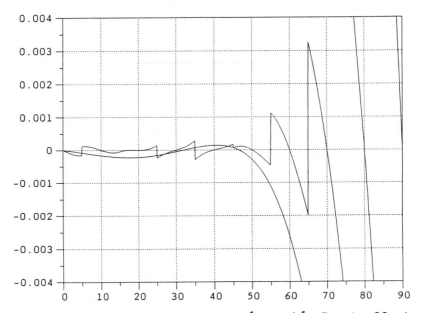

Figure 2.   Error curves (approximation – function) for Equation 22, given by the jagged plot, and Equation 23, the smooth plot, vs. angle in degrees.

A useful aid in jogging the memory is to recall from Equation 22 that the initial slope of the sine function is 0.174. The value of sin 10° is just slightly lower than this because the curve begins to flatten. The value for sin 20° shows some additional flattening.

For those who do not wish to memorize any values of sin **a** at all, we can now backtrack and find a very reasonable approximation of the sine function in the same interval 0° to 54°, although the average error will be significantly greater than that just given.

In the derivation of Equation 22, if we subtract a quantity that is relatively small over the range given, namely

$$\frac{b}{10}\left(\frac{2a + b}{120}\right)$$

we will find that we can derive the approximation,

$$1000 \sin d \approx \frac{d}{10}\left[174.4 - \frac{d(d + 1)}{120}\right] \tag{23}$$

where we have now kept four places in 174.4 because it is more significant here than in Equation 22, where the known values sin **a** "pulled" the curve closer to the correct one.

The error curve for this approximation is also given in Figure 2 as the smooth plot. The error is quite low over the range 0°–54°, but nonetheless it is greater on average than the other.

It is important to recognize that the plots in Figure 2 are designed to accentuate the errors. If the true sine function from 0° to 54° were plotted on a full page here, the difference between it and either of the sine approximations (Equations 22 and 23) would be less than the width of the printed line itself!

Now returning to the quandary that began this entire enterprise, as mentioned in Chapter 1, we can easily find sin 28°. From Equation 22,

$$1000 \sin 28° \approx 1000 \sin 30° - .2 \left(174 - \frac{30 \cdot 28}{40} \right)$$

$$\approx 500 - 30.6$$

or,

$$\sin 28° \approx .4694 \qquad \text{Actual value: .46947} \ldots$$

From Equation 23,

$$1000 \sin 28° \approx 2.8 \left(174.4 - \frac{28 \cdot 29}{120} \right)$$

$$\sin 28° \approx .46937$$

Let us defer the task of finding sin **d** for **d** ≥ 54° and instead address the cosine function. We begin with the identity,

$$\sin (a + b) = \sin a \cos b + \cos a \sin b$$

or,

$$\cos a = \frac{\sin (a + b) - \sin a \cos b}{\sin b}$$

For **b** = 1°, then sin **b** = .01745 and cos **b** = .99985. Substituting our approximation (Equation 22) for sin (**a** + **b**), and setting **b** = 1° yields

$$\cos a \approx 1 - .00014327a(a + 1)$$

Changing **a** to the variable **d** and realizing that 1/7 = .1429 . . . , we find

$$1000 \cos d \approx 1000 - \frac{d(d + 1)}{7} \tag{24}$$

The smooth curve in Figure 3 displays the absolute error (again, approximation − function) for this relation as a function of angle. This approximation shows reasonable accuracy (usually three digits, but rarely more than one off in the third digit) through 40°. A passing familiarity with the hump at around 30° can result in three-digit accuracy throughout this range. This is the formula I

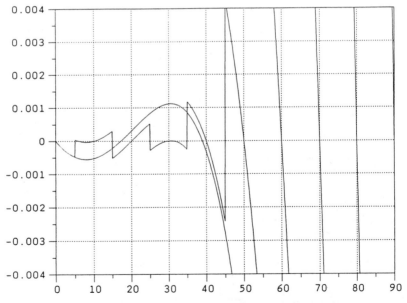

Figure 3. Error curves (approximation − function) for Equation 24, given by the smooth plot, and Equation 25, the jagged plot, vs. angle in degrees.

have used on occasion, and it requires no memorization of cosine values. Using this formula without recalling that we are in the hump area, we find that cos 28° is approximately .8840, compared to the actual value of .8829 . . . .

We can take this formula, however, and form a more uniformly accurate approximation if we memorize the cosines of angles that are again multiples of 10°. For **d** = **a** + **b**, Equation 24 becomes

$$1000 \cos d \approx 1000 - \frac{(a + b) \bullet (a + 1 + b)}{7}$$

Substituting Equation 24 again for cos **a**,

$$1000 \cos d \approx 1000 \cos a - \frac{b(a + d + 1)}{7} \tag{25}$$

The jagged trace in Figure 3 comprises the error curve for this function. It shows an improvement on average over that shown for Equation 24 in the interval $0° \leq d \leq 35°$, assuming that for **d** = 35° we take **a** = 30° and **b** = 5°. To use this relation, we therefore need to know the following values:

cos 0° = 1

cos 10° = .9848

cos 20° = .9397

cos 30° = √3/2 = .8660

With this relation, we find cos 28° as:

$$1000 \cos 28° \approx 1000 \cos 30° - \frac{(-2) \bullet 59}{7}$$

$$\cos 28° \approx .8829$$

which is accurate to four digits.

Nature has been unusually kind to us in both of these relations because the range of angles for which the sine approximations

(Equations 22 and 23) are invalid is almost exactly (or is exactly) the range of angles for which the cosine approximations (Equations 24 and 25) are valid, and vice-versa. Therefore, we can let sin **d** for **d** > 54° become cos (90° − **d**), whose argument is less than 36°, and cos **d** for **d** > 35° become sin (90° − **d**). In the end, we cover the entire 0° to 90° range of interest for both the sine and cosine functions with two formulas. Incidentally, the alternative if this were not true would be to add a third relation, an identity, to double the useful range of the cosine approximation:

$$\cos 2d = 2 \cos^2 d - 1$$

The corresponding double-angle identity for the sine function mixes sine and cosine terms and is not useful.

We may note in closing this sine-cosine discussion that Equations 23 and 24 yield the approximation,

$$\cos d \approx \frac{172 \sin d}{d} - 2$$

For a right triangle with sides of length $a \le b \le c$, we can formulate the above relation to express the smallest angle **A** of the triangle in terms of the three sides [3,4]:

$$A \approx 172 \frac{a}{b + 2c} \tag{26}$$

where **A** is in degrees. The third angle is then apparent.

This approximation was given by Ozanam in 1699 and is actually very good, giving almost four-digit accuracy for angles up to 45° (where the angle is no longer the smallest). For the familiar 3,4,5 right triangle with a smallest angle of 36.870°, this formula gives

$$A \approx 172 \bullet (3/14) \approx 36.857°$$

The Tangent Function

The tangent function, of course, may by definition be calculated by dividing the sine function by the cosine function for the given angle. Since these formulas are not valid in the same range, though, the calculations reduce in practice to:

$$\tan d = \frac{\sin d}{\cos d} \qquad \text{for } 0° \le d < 36°$$

$$= \frac{\sin d}{\sin(90° - d)} \qquad \text{for } 36° \le d \le 54°$$

$$= \frac{\cos(90° - d)}{\sin(90° - d)}, \qquad \text{for } 54° < d \le 90°$$

These need not be remembered, as the proper terms become apparent when performing the individual sine and cosine calculations.

Using the sine relation (Equation 22) and cosine relation (Equation 24), we find tan 28° to be .5310 . . . instead of the actual value of .53171 . . . . Using the cosine relation (Equation 25), we arrive at a value of .53168 . . . .

There exists a power series for tan **x** that can be truncated with relaxed coefficients [5]:

$$\tan x \approx x + .31755x^3 + .20330x^5$$

The magnitude of the error in this approximation is less than 0.001 for the range $0° \le x \le \pi/4$, or 45°. However, the relatively large coefficient of the last term indicates difficulty in further simplification. If we proceed in the same manner as for sin **x**, though, recognizing that the form of the relation is the same, we derive for **d** = **a** + **b**,

$$1000 \tan d \approx 1000 \tan a + \frac{b}{10}\left(174 + \frac{ad}{20}\right) \qquad (27)$$

where we memorize or recall the following values:

$$\tan 0° = 0$$

$$\tan 10° = .1763$$

tan 20° = .3640

tan 30° = √3/3 = .5774

tan 40° = .8391

tan 45° = 1

Note the change in sign of the last term in Equation 27 compared to the earlier sine approximation (Equation 23) of the same form.

The error curve for the approximation (Equation 27) is shown in Figure 4. The increase in difficulty in approximating tan **d** compared to sin **d** or cos **d** is apparent.

Equation 27 can be modified empirically to greatly improve the accuracy, but with additional memorization required:

$$1000 \tan d \approx 1000 \tan a + \frac{b}{10}\left(174 + m + \frac{ad}{20}\right) + \frac{nb^2}{40} \qquad (28)$$

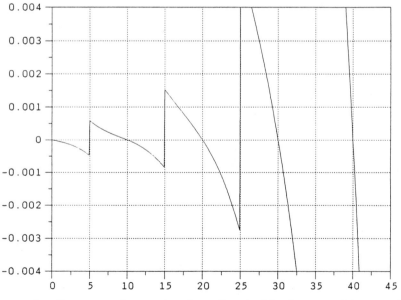

Figure 4.   Error curve (approximation − function) for Equation 27 vs. angle in degrees.

The values of **m** and **n** appear below, where they have been contrived to aid memorization:

a	m	n
0	1	0
10	1.5	0
20	4.5	1
30	15	3
40	45	10

Figure 5 displays the error curve for this approximation, which is for all practical purposes accurate to at least three decimal places (or ± 0.0005) for 0° ≤ **d** ≤ 45°, and requires no significant division.

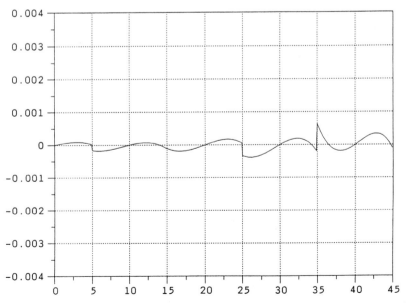

Figure 5. Error curve (approximation – function) for Equation 28 vs. angle in degrees.

Using this formula,

$$1000 \tan 28° \approx 1000 \tan 30° + (-.2) \bullet \left(189 + \frac{28 \bullet 30}{40}\right) + \frac{3 \bullet 4}{40}$$

$$\tan 28° \approx .53145 \ldots$$

compared to the actual value of .53171 . . . .

The range $45° < d \leq 90°$ is very difficult to approximate explicitly because the tangent function tends to infinity. However, for this range we can use the trigonometric identity,

$$\tan d = \frac{1}{\tan (90° - d)}$$

and suffer the division, although with this disadvantage it is probably easier to take the sine-cosine ratio.

The Arcsine and Arccosine Functions

The trigonometric inverses are exceedingly difficult to approximate well mentally, but are not often required in practical work. Looking at Equations 22 through 28, the only one amenable to inversion is the simpler cosine function (Equation 24). The resulting expression for arccos **x** after some simplification is given by

$$\text{arccos } x \approx [7(1000 - 1000x)]^{1/2} - .5 \tag{29}$$

Three identities linking the arcsine and arccosine functions are of use to us here:

$$\text{arccos } x = \text{arcsin } (1 - x^2)^{1/2} \tag{30}$$

$$\text{arcsin } x = \text{arccos } (1 - x^2)^{1/2} \tag{31}$$

$$\text{arcsin } x = 90° - \text{arccos } x \tag{32}$$

We can then substitute the last two of these into Equation 29 to arrive at another relation for arccos **x**:

$$\arccos x \approx 90° - [7(1000 - 1000(1 - x^2)^{1/2})]^{1/2} - .5 \qquad (33)$$

Plots of the absolute error curves for Equations 29 and 33 are given in Figure 6 for $0 \le x \le 1$, or $90° \ge d \ge 0°$, where d = arccos x in degrees. As is evident, Equation 29 provides best results for x above .707 ($d < 45°$) and Equation 33 for the complement. The two relations coincide at $d = 45°$, where $x = (1 - x^2)^{1/2}$.

This pair of formulas yields angles accurate to ± 0.5° over the first quadrant (other quadrants are easily deduced). The square roots are readily found to four or more digits by the methods described in Chapter 3. In fact, the squaring operation here should be more intimidating at this point than the square root extraction. The arcsine can also be easily determined through these relations and the Equations 30–32.

Can we use our memorized values of the sine function to aid in calculating the arcsine (and arccosine) functions? Given that the reader is interested in this abstruse section, we may assume that sine values have been memorized from the last section for the

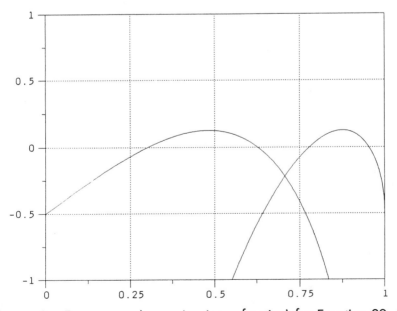

Figure 6. Error curves (approximation – function) for Equation 29, the rightmost plot, and Equation 33, the leftmost plot, vs. the cosine of angles to 90°.

first several multiples of 10°. Now, a series relation for arcsin **x**, where –1 < **x** < 1, exists in a similar form to those of the last section [5]:

$$\text{arcsin } x = x + \frac{x^3}{2 \cdot 3} + \frac{1 \cdot 3 \cdot x^5}{2 \cdot 4 \cdot 5} + \frac{1 \cdot 3 \cdot 5 \cdot x^7}{2 \cdot 4 \cdot 6 \cdot 7} + \dots$$

Truncating this series after the second term, substituting **x** = **a** + **b**, dropping a **b**^{4} term and separating out the terms comprising arcsin **a**, we find

$$\text{arcsin } (a + b) \approx \text{arcsin } a + \frac{401}{7} b \left(1 + \frac{ax}{2}\right) \tag{34}$$

The familiar coefficient 401/7 converts the result into degrees.

The general procedure, then, is to recall the sin **d** value nearest **x** and call it **a**. Then **b** = **x** – **a**. As in general **a** is not a round number, and because we multiply by 401/7, Equation 34 is somewhat more difficult than the corresponding formulas from the last section.

If **x** = .46947, then **a** = .5 = arcsin 30° and **b** = –.03053. Then,

$$\text{arcsin } x \approx 30° + \frac{401}{7} (-.0305) \cdot \left[1 + \frac{(.5)(.46947)}{2}\right]$$

$$\approx 30° - 1.95°$$

$$\approx 28.05°$$

compared to the actual value of 28°.

The error curve for Equation 34 is shown in Figure 7. As expected, the approximation becomes poorer for larger **x**, even though the intervals between values of **a** become smaller. The first 45° range (0 ≤ **x** ≤ .707) is quite acceptable, however, and Equations 30–32 then provide arcsine and arccosine values throughout the first quadrant.

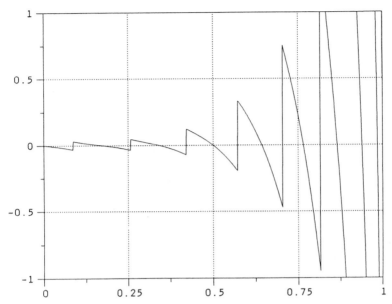

Figure 7. Error curve (approximation – function) for Equation 34 vs. the sine of angles to 90°.

For additional accuracy, we find from Hastings [2] that

$$\arcsin x \approx \pi/2 - (1 - x)^{1/2} \bullet (1.57073 - .21211x$$

$$+ .07426x^2 - .01873x^3)$$

with an error no greater than 0.00005 for $0 \le x \le 1$.

The second term is obviously that for arccos **x**. Since we desire **x** to be as small as possible, let us consider as before the range $0 \le x \le .707$. We can truncate this expression, realizing that we need to multiply by $180/\pi$ to convert arccos **x** into degrees **d**. If we drop terms involving powers of **x** greater than 1, and empirically add a correction term on the end of our resulting relation, we find

$$\arccos x \approx (1 - x)^{1/2} \bullet (90 - 12x) + 1.5(x - .1) \qquad (35)$$

A plot of the error function for this approximation is shown in Figure 8. We deduced earlier from Equations 31–32 that

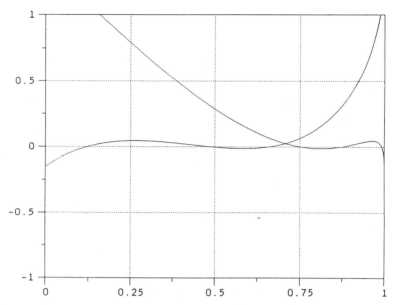

Figure 8. Error curves (approximation – function) for Equation 35, optimized for **x** ≤ .707, and after modifications, optimized for **x** ≥ .707, vs. the cosine of angles to 90°.

arccos **x** = 90° − arccos$(1 - x^2)^{1/2}$. The corresponding error function for this approximation is shown as well in Figure 8, where Equation 35 is again used for approximating the arccosine function. This latter approximation represents the arccosine function with greater accuracy for **x** ≥ .707.

With Equations 30–32, we have covered the first quadrant for the arcsine and arccosine functions to reasonable accuracy, given the infrequency of the situation. Taking again the example **x** = .4694716,

arccos x ≈ 62.0044°

compared to the actual value of 90° − 28° = 62°.

It is also worth mentioning more exact approximations (in some regions) for arcsin **x** and arccos **x** formulated from our earlier approximation (Equation 26) for the smallest angle **A** in a right triangle of sides a ≤ b ≤ c. If we define a = x and c = 1, then **A** = arcsin (a/c) = arcsin **x**. Writing b = $(c^2 - a^2)^{1/2}$ = $(1 - x^2)^{1/2}$

and replacing the number 172 by 3(401/7), we arrive at the expression,

$$\arcsin x \approx \frac{3x}{2 + (1 - x^2)^{1/2}} \cdot \left(\frac{401}{7}\right) \tag{36}$$

Likewise, setting $b = x$, $c = 1$, and $a = (1 - x^2)^{1/2}$, we find

$$\arccos x \approx \frac{3(1 - x^2)^{1/2}}{x + 2} \cdot \left(\frac{401}{7}\right) \tag{37}$$

An alternative means of deriving these relations uses the accelerated Borchardt's Algorithm described in Chapter 4 [6]. To the iterative relations given there, we apply the initial values $a_0 = (1 - x^2)^{1/2}$ and $g_0 = 1$ and produce approximations for the arcsine function, the first being Equation 36. Setting $a_0 = x$ and $g_0 = 1$ produces approximations for the arccosine function, the first given by Equation 37.

We find here that the result for the arcsine function is identical to that obtained by transforming x in the arccosine formula by $(1 - x^2)^{1/2}$. The error curves for Equations 36 and 37 are plotted in Figure 9. Choosing the more accurate equation and, if necessary, using the earlier identities gives the best accuracy yet for these functions, albeit at the expense of more difficult computations. Perhaps these relations are best left to cases where x is a value of one or two digits.

The Arctangent Function

One approach to approximating the arctangent function utilizes the following relation [5], with the multiplier again added for conversion to degrees:

$$\arctan x \approx \frac{401}{7} \cdot \frac{x}{1 + .28x^2} \tag{38}$$

for $-1 \leq x \leq 1$. A plot of the corresponding error function is shown in Figure 10, showing an absolute error less than 0.28° over the

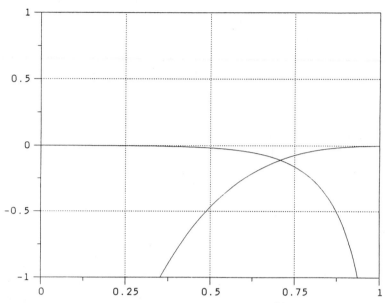

Figure 9.   Error curves (approximation – function) for Equation 36, the leftmost plot, and Equation 37, the rightmost plot, vs. **x**.

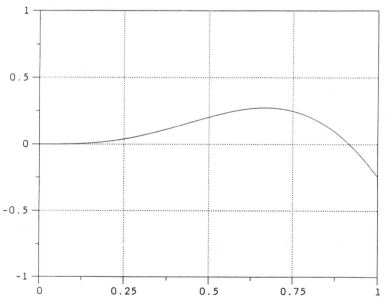

Figure 10.   Error curve (approximation – function) for Equation 38 vs. the tangent of angles to 45°.

range $-1 \leq x \leq 1$, or $0° \leq d \leq 45°$, where d = arctan x in degrees. A potential difficulty exists for the range $45° \leq d \leq 90°$, however, as the arctangent function careens to infinity. The solution is to use the identity,

$$\text{arctan } x = 90° - \text{arctan } (1/x) \tag{39}$$

to reduce x in this region to a value less than 1. To avoid excess computations, we can replace x in Equation 38 with $1/x$ and simplify, giving

$$\text{arctan } x \approx 90° - \frac{401}{7} \bullet \frac{x}{x^2 + .28} \tag{40}$$

for $x > 1$.

Another method makes use of memorized values of tan d for d = 0°, 10°, 20°, 30°, 40°, and 45°, as given in the discussion on the tangent function. If these values are memorized for calculating tan d, they may be used here as well to great advantage.

The derivation follows from an identity for the tangent function [7]. For $x = a + b$,

$$\tan d = x$$

$$\tan e = a$$

$$\tan (d - e) = \frac{\tan d - \tan e}{1 + \tan d \tan e} = \frac{x - a}{1 + ax}$$

or,

$$d = \text{arctan } a + \text{arctan } \left(\frac{b}{1 + a(a + b)} \right)$$

For small arguments of the last term, we arrive at

$$\text{arctan } x \approx \text{arctan } a + \frac{401}{7} \bullet \frac{b}{1 + ax} \tag{41}$$

for $x = a + b$.

A plot of the error function for $0 \leq x \leq 1$ is given in Figure 11. Notice the order of magnitude change in the scale; this is an extremely accurate approximation with little increase in complexity over the last, given the memorization required. Again, Equation 39 is used for $x > 1$.

For those interested, Equation 26 can be used to derive an extremely accurate approximation to the arctangent function as well as the earlier arcsine and arccosine functions. We derive:

$$\arctan x \approx \frac{3x}{1 + 2(1 + x^2)^{1/2}} \bullet \frac{401}{7}$$

The accelerated Borchardt's Algorithm can also be used to derive this; the initial values used here for the arctangent function are given as $a_0 = 1$, $g_0 = (1 + x^2)^{1/2}$.

The extreme accuracy of this relation for $0 \leq x \leq 1$ seems unnecessary considering the accuracy available from the previous relation.

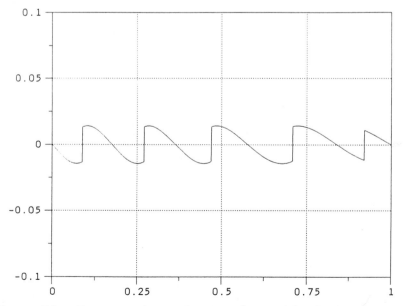

Figure 11. Error curve (approximation – function) for Equation 41 vs. the tangent of angles to 45°.

Other Approximations

Many other approximations exist for trigonometric and inverse trigonometric functions. However, the vast majority do not lend themselves even as well as the ones given here to mental (or back of the envelope) solution. For those interested, references for other approximations include Fike [8], Kogbetliantz [9–12], Fox [13], Frame [14], and Spielberg [15].

Interestingly enough, mental calculation of hyperbolic and inverse hyperbolic trigonometric functions (an extremely impressive talent) is much easier, since they are simply defined in terms of real exponential and logarithmic functions more readily evaluated by the methods of the last chapter. For example,

$$2 \text{ arctanh } x = \log (1 + x) - \log (1 - x)$$

Other relations are easily found from definitions of these functions.

Bibliography

1. Rudolf Flesch, *The Book of Unusual Quotations*, Harper and Brothers, New York, 1957, p. 252.
2. Cecil Hastings, Jr., *Approximations for Digital Computers*, Princeton University Press, Princeton, 1955, pp. 138, 159.
3. Roger A. Johnson, "Determination of an Angle of a Right Triangle, without Tables," *American Mathematical Monthly, 27* (1920) pp. 368–369.
4. J. S. Frame, "Solving a Right Triangle without Tables," *American Mathematical Monthly, 50* (1943), pp. 622–623.
5. M. Abromowitz and I. A. Stegun, *Handbook of Mathematical Functions*, Applied Mathematics Series, Vol. 55, National Bureau of Standards, Washington, 1964, reprinted by Dover Publications, New York, 1972, pp. 76, 81.
6. B. C. Carlson, "An Algorithm for Computing Logarithms and Arctangents," *Mathematics of Computation, 26* (1972) pp. 543–549.
7. John Szymanski, "On Arctan (**A** + **B**)," *The Mathematical Gazette, 68* (1984) pp. 121–122.
8. C. T. Fike, *Computer Evaluation of Mathematical Functions*, Prentice-Hall, Englewood Cliffs, 1968.

9. E. G. Kogbetliantz, "Computation of Sin **N**, Cos **N** and $^m\sqrt{N}$ Using an Electronic Computer," *IBM Journal of Research and Development, 3* (1959) pp. 147–152.

10. E. G. Kogbetliantz, "Computation of Arcsin **N** for $0 < N < 1$ Using an Electronic Computer," *IBM Journal of Research and Development, 2* (1958) pp. 218–222.

11. E. G. Kogbetliantz, "Computation of Arctan **N** for $-\infty < N < +\infty$ Using an Electronic Computer," *IBM Journal of Research and Development, 2* (1958) pp. 43–53.

12. E. G. Kogbetliantz, "Generation of Elementary Functions," in *Mathematical Methods for Digital Computers* (ed. Anthony Ralston and Herbert Wilf), John Wiley and Sons, New York, 1960, pp. 7–35.

13. Michael Fox, "Quick Padé Approximations," *The Mathematical Gazette, 69* (1985) pp. 21–25.

14. J. S. Frame, "A Trigonometric Approximation," *American Mathematical Monthly, 53* (1946) p. 454.

15. Kurt Spielberg, "Efficient Continued Fraction Approximations to Elementary Functions," *Mathematics of Computation, 15* (1961) pp. 409–417.

Concluding Remarks

The object of pure Physic is the unfolding of the laws of the intelligible world; the object of pure Mathematic that of unfolding the laws of human intelligence.

J. J. Sylvester [1]

To think the thinkable—that is the mathematician's aim.

C. J. Keyser (1904) [1]

This, then, represents a collection of algorithms specifically developed for mentally calculating or approximating arithmetic results and elementary functions. I hope that a sense of adventure and marvel has been conveyed, and a certain eagerness inspired to try out the techniques as the opportunity arises or is created.

I also strongly recommend looking through the referenced articles and books for more detailed information on any topic that piques your interest. I appreciate that this may be an unfamiliar step for some people; it shouldn't be, and the majority of the references can be found in the library of even a small college or obtained through any public library. The many articles and books listed are clear ones and are certainly within the grasp of anyone who appreciates the topics in this book. Some of them, including those by Mermin [2], Goldstine [3], Taylor [4], Menninger [5], Aitken [6], Loweke [7], Uspensky [8], Eynden [9], Bailey [10], and Kovach [11] (in no particular order) are simply a pleasure to read. As you may have gathered, Smith's book on mental calculators [12], which has a somewhat different emphasis, complements this book very nicely.

One important fact implicit in the presentation of the methods in this book is that they are in no way the final word on the subject. I encourage the reader to find better and alternate methods. Experimenting with perceived properties of numbers or functions can be done at any odd time on any scrap of paper, and this is an area where playing with particular numbers often leads to general algebraic relationships or approximations. It invariably leads to some insight into the intricacies of the number world. Hoist a sail and catch the wind.

Bibliography

1. Robert E. Moritz, *Memorabilia Mathematica*, Macmillan, New York, 1914, pp. 7, 134.
2. N. David Mermin, "Logarithms!," *American Journal of Physics*, 46 (1978) pp. 101–105.
3. Herman H. Goldstine, *A History of Numerical Analysis From the 16th Through the 19th Century*, Springer-Verlag, New York, 1977.
4. L. F. Taylor, *Numbers*, Faber and Faber, London, 1970.
5. Karl Menninger, *Calculator's Cunning*, Basic Books, New York, 1964.
6. A. C. Aitken, "The Art of Mental Calculation; with Demonstrations," *Transactions of the Society of Engineers*, 44 (1954) pp. 295–309.
7. George P. Loweke, *The Lore of Prime Numbers*, Vantage, New York, 1982.
8. J. V. Uspensky, *Theory of Equations*, McGraw-Hill, New York, 1948.
9. Charles Vanden Eynden, "Flipping a Coin over the Telephone," *Mathematics Magazine*, 62 (1989) pp. 167–172.
10. D. F. Bailey, "A Historical Survey of Solution by Functional Iteration," *Mathematics Magazine*, 62 (1989) pp. 155–166.

11. Ladis D. Kovach, "Ancient Algorithms Adapted to Modern Computers," *Mathematics Magazine, 37* (1964) pp. 159–165.
12. Steven B. Smith, *The Great Mental Calculators*, Columbia University Press, New York, 1983.

Finding Rational Approximations to Precomputed Constants

The employment of mathematical symbols is perfectly natural when the relations between magnitudes are under discussion; and even if they are not rigorously necessary, it would hardly be reasonable to reject them, because they are not equally familiar to all readers and because they have sometimes been wrongly used, if they are able to facilitate the exposition of problems, to render it more concise, to open the way to more extended developments, and to avoid the digressions of vague argumentation.

A. Cournot (1897) [1]

Often we encounter multidigit numbers, such as scaling factors, which are difficult to use directly as a divisor or multiplier. In addition, there are certain types of calculations, such as those for finding antilogarithms, that benefit from range reduction techniques, i.e., the original number is reduced in some manner into a range where we can obtain a good approximation. We then adjust this approximation to find that for the original number. This whole process generally involves multiplications or divisions by constants (such as $10^{1/2n}$, where n is an integer) that are precomputed and memorized. This appendix describes the general procedure by which we can generate whole-number fractions that approximate multidigit numbers to a required accuracy and in practice involve multiplication and division by reasonably small whole numbers.

To illustrate, to convert from radian units to degrees, we multiply by $180/\pi = 57.296\ldots$ This is difficult to do, and in Chapter 5 I use instead the multiplier $401/7 = 57.286\ldots$ This is a fraction containing numbers that are easy to multiply and divide by, yet is very close to the actual conversion factor. More accurate fractions are $974/17$ and $4068/71$; worse ones include $172/3$ and $229/4$. These approximations are straightforward, but tedious, to generate, so I use a computer program to create them. I then look over them to find one that is a reasonable approximation, but that has a numerator and denominator that I can mentally multiply and divide by relatively easily. Once a fraction (such as $401/7$) is selected, I always use it for this constant in any calculation that requires it.

We approach this subject in terms of interesting creatures called continued fractions. A continued fraction is a fraction of the form:

$$a_1 + \cfrac{1}{a_2 + \cfrac{1}{a_3 + \cfrac{1}{a_4 + \ldots}}}$$

where the integers a_n are termed partial quotients. A more modern notation for continued fractions is given by the equivalent form,

$$a_1 + \cfrac{1}{a_2} + \cfrac{1}{a_3} + \cfrac{1}{a_4} + \ldots$$

A comprehensive treatment of continued fractions may be found in the work of Olds [2]; here we are interested in their application to rational approximations [3,4].

As examples, it is commonly given that:

$$e = 2 + \cfrac{1}{1 +} \cfrac{1}{2 +} \cfrac{1}{1 +} \cfrac{1}{1 +} \cfrac{1}{4 +} \cdots$$

$$\pi = 3 + \cfrac{1}{7 +} \cfrac{1}{15 +} \cfrac{1}{1 +} \cfrac{1}{292 +} \cdots$$

For integer values of a, the continued fraction will converge to a limiting value. Terminating the fraction at given a_n's and simplifying the fraction produces rational approximations to the value called the principal convergents A_n.

We need, therefore, a procedure for converting a given number into a sequence of numbers a_n that comprise a continued fraction for the number. We can extract the principal convergents A_n until we arrive at fractions involving numbers too large for us to work with. Convenient fractions can then be tested for accuracy to the original number. As a rule, we expect good approximations for a given complexity of the fraction to occur when the next a_n following termination is relatively large, as its reciprocal would provide a correspondingly small correction if included. For example, in the continued fraction for π given earlier, terminating the fraction at a_4 (before $a_5 = 292$) gives 355/113, a value accurate to 7 digits. Finally, we can find intermediate convergents; these occur for any principal convergent A_n that results from truncating the continued fraction at a partial quotient a_0 greater than 1.

It can be shown that the values a_n are simply the multipliers in each step of Euclid's Algorithm for finding the greatest common divisor of two integers (see Chapter 2). To prove this, consider two numbers a and b with $a > b$. Euclid's Algorithm gives:

$a = a_1 b + r_1$

$b = a_2 r_1 + r_2$

$r_1 = a_3 r_2 + r_3$

   etc.

Dividing each line by the variable associated with the a_n term, we find

$$\frac{a}{b} = a_1 + \frac{r_1}{b}$$

$$\frac{b}{r_1} = a_2 + \frac{r_2}{r_1}$$

$$\frac{r_1}{r_2} = a_3 + \frac{r_3}{r_2}$$

etc.

Then, since the last term in each line is the reciprocal of the first term in the next, we have

$$\frac{a}{b} = a_1 + \cfrac{1}{a_2 + \cfrac{r_2}{r_1}}$$

$$= a_1 + \cfrac{1}{a_2 + \cfrac{1}{a_3 + \cfrac{r_3}{r_2}}}$$

etc.

Now, to approximate a constant, we convert it to an integer fraction by letting **a** equal the constant stripped of its decimal point and carried to **d** digits, and letting **b** equal $10^{(d-1)}$. As a pertinent example from Chapter 4, let us find rational approximations to $10^{1/16} = 1.154782\ldots.$ Taking $a = 1154782$ and $b = 1000000$, we proceed as follows:

$$1154782 = 1(1000000) + 154782$$

$$1000000 = 6(154782) + 71308$$

$$154782 = 2(71308) + 12166$$

$71308 = 5(12166) + 10478$

$12166 = 1(10478) + 1688$

$10478 = 6(1688) + 350$

$1688 = 4(350) + 288$

Stopping at this point, we have obtained the partial quotients $a_1 = 1$, $a_2 = 6$, $a_3 = 2$, $a_4 = 5$, $a_5 = 1$, $a_6 = 6$, and $a_7 = 4$.
These are used to determine the principal convergents A_n:

$$A_1 = a_1 = 1$$

$$A_2 = a_1 + \frac{1}{a_2} = 7/6$$

Actually, at this point we can ease our work by realizing that for $A_n = p_n/q_n$,

$$p_n = a_n p_{n-1} + p_{n-2}$$

$$q_n = a_n q_{n-1} + q_{n-2}$$

and we can continue quite rapidly:

$$A_3 = \frac{2 \bullet 7 + 1}{2 \bullet 6 + 1} = \frac{15}{13}$$

$$A_4 = \frac{5 \bullet 15 + 7}{5 \bullet 13 + 6} = \frac{82}{71}$$

$$A_5 = \frac{97}{84} \; ; \quad A_6 = \frac{664}{575} \; ; \quad A_7 = \frac{2753}{2384}$$

Now there are intermediate convergents as well between A_{n-2} and A_n for each $a_n > 1$. These are of the form:

$$\frac{p_{n-2}}{q_{n-2}} = A_{n-2}$$

$$\frac{p_{n-2} + p_{n-1}}{q_{n-2} + q_{n-1}}$$

$$\frac{p_{n-2} + 2p_{n-1}}{q_{n-2} + 2q_{n-1}}$$

$$\ldots$$

$$\ldots$$

$$\ldots$$

$$\frac{p_{n-2} + a_n p_{n-1}}{q_{n-2} + a_n q_{n-1}} = A_n$$

Representing the intermediate convergents as $(A_{n-2} \ A_n)$, we find

$$a_3 = 2: \ (A_1 A_3) = \frac{1 + 7}{1 + 6} = \frac{8}{7}$$

$$a_4 = 5: \ (A_2 A_4) = \frac{7 + 15}{6 + 13} = \frac{22}{19}, \frac{37}{32}, \frac{52}{45}, \frac{67}{58}$$

$a_5 = 1$: no intermediate convergents as $a_n \leq 1$

$$a_6 = 6: \ (A_4 A_6) = \frac{82 + 97}{71 + 84} = \frac{179}{155}, \frac{276}{239}, \frac{373}{323}, \frac{470}{407}, \frac{567}{491}$$

$$a_7 = 4: \ (A_5 A_7) = \frac{97 + 664}{84 + 575} = \frac{761}{659}, \frac{1425}{1234}, \frac{2089}{1809}$$

Here we find those principal convergents we would get if we allowed subtractions instead of additions in various steps of Euclid's Algorithm.

In the end, we arrive at two convergent sequences. The first one increases, approaching $10^{1/16}$ from below, and consists of the odd principal convergents and their intermediate convergents:

$$A_1, (A_1A_3), A_3, A_5, (A_5A_7), A_7$$

or,

$$1, \frac{8}{7}, \frac{15}{13}, \frac{97}{84}, \frac{761}{659}, \frac{1425}{1234}, \frac{2089}{1809}, \frac{2753}{2384}$$

The second sequence decreases, approaching $10^{1/16}$ from above, and consists of the even principal convergents and their intermediate convergents:

$$A_2, (A_2A_4), A_4, (A_4A_6), A_6$$

or,

$$\frac{7}{6}, \frac{22}{19}, \frac{37}{32}, \frac{52}{45}, \frac{67}{58}, \frac{82}{71}, \frac{179}{155}, \frac{276}{239}, \frac{373}{323}, \frac{470}{407}, \frac{567}{491}, \frac{664}{575}$$

A computer provides, of course, a convenient means of tabulating these fractions, as it did for me.

Now we have the intriguing task of choosing a fraction that provides good accuracy with a convenient numerator and denominator for multiplication (we flip the fraction for division). Since a_2, a_4, and a_6 are relatively large, we are clued to look at A_1, A_3, and A_5 for proximity to 1.154782 relative to their complexity. We discover

$$A_1 = 1$$

$$A_3 = 15/13 = 1.1538462\ldots$$

$$A_5 = 97/84 = 1.1547619\ldots$$

Perusing other choices reveals 52/45 = 104/90 as a possibility, but its accuracy is poor (1.1555555 . . .). Therefore, perhaps our best pick, particularly in light of the factoring available for cancellation when additional constants are multiplied or divided, is:

$$10^{1/16} \approx 97/84$$

$$\approx \frac{100 - 3}{3 \bullet 4 \bullet 7}$$

$$\approx 1.154762 \text{ compared to } 1.154782\ldots$$

This rational approximation appears in Table 8.

Bibliography

1. Robert E. Moritz, *Memorabilia Mathematica*, Macmillan, New York, 1914, p. 199.
2. Carl D. Olds, *Continued Fractions*, Random House, New York, 1963.
3. Paul D. Thomas, "Approximations to Incommensurable Numbers by Ratios of Positive Integers," *Mathematics Magazine*, 36 (1963) pp. 281–289.
4. Hans Riesel, *Prime Numbers and Computer Methods for Factorization*, Birkhäuser, Boston, 1985, pp. 300–307.

Index

Addition, 9–10
Aitken, Alexander Craig, 5, 35,
    77, 79
Algebraic factors, 54–56
Antilogarithms, 133ff
    Bemer's method for, 137–42
    Brigg's method for, 133–37
    definition of, 114, 113
Arccosine, 156-62
    Borchardt's Algorithm for,
        160–62
    method with table for, 157–58
    method without table for,
        156–57
    precise method without table
        for, 159–160
Arcsine, 156–62
    Borchardt's Algorithm for,
        160–62
    method with table for, 157–58
    method without table for,
        156–57
    precise method without table
        for, 159–60
Arctangent, 161–64
    Borchardt's Algorithm for, 164

method with table for, 163–64
method without table for,
    161–63

Bidder, George Parker, 117
Borchardt's Algorithm, 130-33,
    161, 164
Briggs, Henry, 116, 133–34

Chebyshev, P. L., 86
Composite numbers, 47. *See also*
    Prime numbers.
Computers
    Bemer's logarithm method on,
        137
    binary, 3, 38, 18, 132
    decimal, 3, 96, 137
    factoring methods on, 68
    hexadecimal test for, 45
    precomputing constants with,
        177
Continued fractions, 172–78
    definition of, 172
    rational approximations using,
        173–78

Cosine, 149–52
  method with table for, 151
  method without table for,
    149–51
Cournot, A., 171
Cross multiplication, 11
Cube roots, particular methods
  for, 99–104. *See also* Roots.
Cubing, 17–18. *See also*
  Multiplication.

Degrees, conversion to radians,
  146, 172
Divisibility, 39ff
  by numbers with multiple near
    power of ten, 41–42
  by odd numbers, 42–44
  by particular numbers, 40–42,
    45–46
  elevens test for, 40
  Euclid's Algorithm for, 44
  factoring sieves using, 72–73
  nines test for, 39–40
  other bases for, 45–47
Division, 19ff. *See also* Divisibility.
  by factors of numbers near
    round numbers, 28
  by numbers near round
    numbers, 24–28
  a cross (or Fourier), 28–33, 97
  repeating decimals and,
    19–24, 35

Error checking, 39ff. *See also*
  Divisibility.
Euclid's Algorithm. *See also*
  Greatest common divisor.
  continued fractions and,
    173–78
  definition of, 35–38

divisibility tests with, 44–45
factoring with, 65
Euler, factoring methods of,
  61–65.

Factorization, 47ff
  Euler's method of, 61–65
  Fermat's method of, 48–54,
    68–73
  general Euler's method of, 65
  Legendre's method of, 54–56
  Triangular number method of,
    57–61, 65–66, 73
  Vaes' method of, 56–57
Fermat, Pierre de, 48, 54, 61
Fifth roots, particular methods
  for, 105–108. *See also* Roots.
Finger counting, 12
Fourier, Joseph, 28, 97

Greatest common divisor, 35ff
  Euclid's Algorithm for, 35–36
  halving method for, 38
  least–remainder method for, 36
  modified Euclid's Algorithm
    for, 37–38

Halley, Edmond, 83, 107, 123
Hexadecimal error checking,
  45–46
Hofstadter, Douglas R., 4–5
Hyperbolic trigonometric
  functions, methods for, 165

Inverse logarithms. *See* Antilogarithms.
Inverse trigonometric functions,
  156ff. *See also* Arccosine;
  Arcsine; Arctangent.

Keyser, C. J., 167
Knuth, Donald E., 18, 48
Kogbetliantz, E. G., 113

Lagrange interpolation, 129–30
Legendre, A. M., factoring
    method of, 54–56
Lightning calculators
    methods of, 11, 18, 20–21, 24,
        35, 44, 62, 77–79, 117–18
    names of, 4–5, 117
    performance of, 3–5
Logarithms, 113ff
    Bidder's method for, 117–18
    Borchardt's Algorithm for,
        130–33
    definition of, 114–15
    factoring for, 40
    Halley's method for, 123–26
    Lagrange's formula applied to,
        129–30
    neighboring value methods for,
        121–23
    Newton's method for, 126–28
    prime number, 119–21
    root extraction using, 142–144
    series approximation for,
        116–17
Lowell, James Russell, 1
Lowest common multiple, 39

Melding, 6–8
Mental calculators. *See* Lightning
    calculators.
Modular arithmetic
    identities in, 35–36
    sieves using, 50–56, 59–61, 64,
        68–73
Multiplication, 10–18. *See also*
    Cubing; Squaring.

cross, 11
distributive law method of, 11
large number, 18, 47
particular simplifications in,
    12–15

Napier, John, 113, 116
Newton, Isaac, 87, 101, 126
Notation
    mod, 26, 36
    pi, 129
    sigma, 29, 129
    vertical bar, 6–8, 10, 89

Ozanam, triangle relation of, 152,
    160

Prime numbers. *See also*
    Factorization.
    definition of, 19, 48
    fundamental theorem of
        arithmetic and, 47–48
    logarithms of, 118–121 rough
        test for, 66–68
    sums of squares of, 61–62
Primitives, 9ff
    definition of, 9

Quadratic residues, 50

Radians, conversion to degrees,
    146, 172
Rational approximations, 171ff
Reciprocals. *See also* Division.
    approximations to, 33–34
    calculation of, 19–24
    square roots of, 97–99
Roots, 77ff. *See also* Cube roots;
    Fifth roots; Square roots.

Chebyshev's correction for,
  86–87, 98–99, 100–102,
  105
general algorithm for square,
  87–97
Halley's method for, 83–85, 98,
  100, 105
integer, 77–79
Newton–Raphson method for,
  80–83, 97–99, 103–105
particular methods for cube,
  99–104
particular methods for fifth and
  higher, 105–108
particular methods for square,
  79–87, 98
reciprocal square, 97–99
use of logarithms for, 115,
  142–44
Russell, Bertrand, 145

Sine, 145–52
method with table for, 146–48
method without table for,
  148–149
Smith, Steven B., 3–4, 44, 79
Square roots, 77–99. *See also*
  Roots.
approximation for reciprocal,
  97–99

general algorithm for, 87–97
particular methods for, 79–87
Wallis' extraction of, 109
Squares
endings of, 49
endings of differences of, 69
sieves for, 50–52, 69–70
Squaring, 15–17. *See also*
  Multiplication.
Subtraction, 9–10
Sylvester, J. J., 167

Tangent, 152–156
general formula for, 153–54
precise formula for, 154–56
sine/cosine method for, 152
Triangular numbers
definition of, 57–58
endings of, 59
factoring methods using,
  57–61, 65–66, 73
sieves for, 59–61
Trigonometric functions, 145ff.
  See also Cosine; Sine;
  Tangent.

Vaes, factoring method of, 56–57

Wallis, John, 5, 109
Whitehead, Alfred North, 9